THE YORK ASSOCIATES TEACHING BUSINESS ENGLISH HANDBOOK

Nick Brieger

York Associates Publications

Copyright © 1997 Nick Brieger

All rights reserved. No part of this publication may be reproduced, stored in a retrieval system, or transmitted in any form or by any means, electronic, mechanical, photocopying, recording, or otherwise, without the prior permission of the publishers.

Published by York Associates, 116 Micklegate, York YO1 1JY, England.
Tel: (0)1904 624246, Fax: (0)1904 646971, E-mail: training@yorkassoc.go-ed.com
Design: Hutton Peach Design Consultants, Newton-on-Ouse, York.
Page setting: Celtic Publishing Services, Ty Brethyn, Llangollen, Denbighshire.
Printed by: Bookcraft (Bath) Ltd., Midsomer Norton.

This book is sold subject to the condition that it shall not, by way of trade or otherwise, be lent, re-sold, hired out or otherwise circulated without the publisher's prior consent in any form of binding or cover than that in which it is published and without a similar condition including this condition being imposed upon the subsequent purchaser.

ISBN 1 900991 07 1
First published in 1997

ABOUT THE AUTHOR

After a first degree in law, a post-graduate teacher training qualification in TEFL and an M.A. in Applied Linguistics, Nick Brieger began to specialise in professional language and communication training, especially in the field of Business English. He joined York Associates as a partner in 1987 and now divides his time between training (in the UK and continental Europe), materials development (both in-house and for commercial publication) and Business English teacher training. He is a regular contributor to international conferences, particularly in the field of ESP.

Nick is the co-author of three series of ESP teaching materials for Phoenix ELT. The *Contacts* series develops language knowledge and skills for learners from business and technical backgrounds at pre-intermediate level and above. The *Business Management English* series develops management knowledge and professional language and communication skills for learners at post-intermediate level and above. *The Language of Business English* series provides reference and practice in core language areas in Business English. In addition, Nick is also the editor of the *Penguin Business English* series.

ABOUT THE PUBLISHER

York Associates is a partnership of five experienced trainers and materials developers, founded in 1980 and based in York in the UK. The company provides one-to-one and small group courses in professional language, communications skills, inter-cultural communication and management training to many major British and European companies both at its own training centres in York and throughout the rest of the world. It also provides teacher training courses world-wide for new and experienced teachers of Business English. It has a sister company, Language Works, in Kuala Lumpur, Malaysia.

Its partners are also all well-known writers and count major series for the BBC, Berlitz, Oxford University Press, Prentice Hall and Penguin among the forty or so training titles so far published between them. York Associates also produces its own specialist and innovative range of video and audio packs and books.

Contents

Foreword by Jeremy Comfort — v
Acknowledgements — vi

Introduction — vii

Part 1: Background Issues In Business And Business English

1	**Introduction to Business English**	
	The scope of teaching Business English	3
	Teachers of Business English	10
	Learners of Business English	12
	Business English versus General English: some contrasts	15
2	**Dealing with Professional Content**	
	Content – the contentious issue	16
	Organisations in business	18
	The evolution of management	19
	The division of labour	24
	Key issues in management	28
	Business sectors	33
3	**The Language of Business English**	
	Grammar	35
	Vocabulary	37
4	**Communication Skills in Business**	
	Accuracy, fluency and effectiveness	39
	Presentations	43
	Meetings	47
	Telephoning	54
	Negotiations	57
	Written documentation	63
5	**Management Skills in Business**	
	Leadership	69
	Team building	71
	Delegation	75
6	**Communication across Cultures**	80

PART 2: PEDAGOGIC ISSUES FOR TEACHING BUSINESS ENGLISH

7   Pre-Course
    Needs analysis and course objectives   87
    Assessing entry levels   99
    Programme outline and trainee briefing   102
8   On Course
    Planning a lesson   104
    Learning styles   108
    Giving feedback   110
    One-to-one teaching and group teaching   117
    Teaching or training?   121
    The scope of materials and equipment   127
9   End of Course
    Ending the course   132
    Reviewing the course   139
    Drafting the course report   144

PART 3: CHECKLISTS

1   Further reading   153
2   Professional development for teachers of Business English   154
3   Published materials in Business English   155
4   Other sources of material for Business English   160
5   Business English examinations   161
6   Language for effective communication   169
    - Presentations
    - Meetings
    - Telephoning
    - Negotiation
7   Areas of specialist vocabulary   180
    - General management
    - Administration
    - Customer service
    - Distribution
    - Finance
    - Legal
    - Marketing
    - Human resources
    - Production and operations
    - Purchasing
    - Research and development
    - Sales

Abbreviations   188
References   188
Index   189

Foreword

Nick Brieger and I started teaching Business English in the late seventies. We felt like pioneers when we started to develop job-specific courses for a frighteningly wide range of students: one week it was Vietnamese trainees learning about the Swedish paper industry; the next, German Sales Managers from one of the big multinationals. Since that time, Business English has grown into a major arm of ELT and an industry in itself. Books, audio and video tapes have proliferated and language schools offering Executive courses have blossomed.

However, perhaps because of the entrepreneurial nature of this area of ELT, teacher training has not developed to support teachers as in other more academic areas. There are now signs that this is being remedied. Nick himself has been instrumental in developing the LCCI CertTEB course delivered by York Associates. He has had the chance to pilot it with teachers in St Petersburg, Tashkent, Warsaw, Budapest, Paris and the UK. It was a relatively small step to go on to develop this handbook. The handbook represents a distillation of Nick's experience in Business English over the last twenty years. For teachers I am sure it will be seen as an ideal introduction to an area which can be daunting.

Nick has set out to meet teachers' needs in two major areas. The first, to develop background knowledge about business, will prove invaluable both for those just entering the profession, and for those who have been teaching for a couple of years but feel uncertain in some areas of business. While teachers should not be expected to be experts in business, they do need to understand what their students do or are training to do. Once teachers have a sound grasp of what makes businesses work, they can develop more relevant courses, plan more motivating lessons and ask more intelligent questions.

The other major concern of the handbook is to develop teaching skills. Business English is becoming a more and more demanding profession. Not only must we cope with our role as language teachers, we must also improve our students' communication skills, increase their cross-cultural sensitivity and develop skills in managing people internationally. The handbook will help to open eyes and doors for both inexperienced and experienced teachers in all these fields.

Nick has brought to this book his unparalleled experience of ESP and Business English as well as his love of teacher training. I feel confident that all Business English teachers will find this an invaluable support.

Jeremy Comfort
York Associates

Acknowledgements

The author and publisher are grateful for the following permissions:

- The Columbia Dictionary of Quotations for the quotations on pages vii–viii of the Introduction. The Columbia Dictionary of Quotations is licensed from Columbia University Press. Copyright © 1993 by Columbia University Press. All rights reserved.
- Paul Smith of Paul Smith Associates, Munich for the Liaison Committee meeting agenda in chapter 4
- Prentice-Hall Inc., Upper Saddle River, NJ for the adaptation of the text on Behavioural Approaches and Context-based Models (up to point 6) in the section on Leadership in Chapter 5, from *Management* (sixth edition) by Stoner, Freeman and Gilbert, © 1991.
- Michael P. O'Connor, The Old Stone House, Dingle, Ireland, for the extract on Team Building from the MNM *Team Building Process for Printers* in chapter 5. © 1996 Michael P. O'Connor. Information about this book is available from Michael P. O'Connor or Becky Erickson, The Old Stone House, Dingle, Ireland, tel / fax: + 353 66 59882, e-mail: moconnor@iol.ie or from COS Group International, 237 Oxford Street, Suite 25F, Portland, Maine 04101, tel: + 1 207 871 8803, fax: + 1 207 883 1340
- International Management Centres, Castle Street, Buckingham MK18 1BP for the extract on Delegation from page 75 to the end of How to Delegate? on page 78. More information about their MBA management training resources in the area of delegation can be found in Time Management Resource Level 3, Time Management and Delegation Resource at: http://www.mcb.co.uk/services/coursewa/mba/mb8.htm#session4
- John Mole and Nicolas Brealey Publishing for the Mole map in Chapter 6, reproduced from *Mind Your Manners: Managing Business Cultures in Europe* by John Mole (1995) published by Nicholas Brealey Publishing, 36 John Street, London WC1N, price £9.99.
- Addison Wesley Longman Ltd and The English Speaking Union for permission to reprint the language scale on pages 100-101 from Carroll B and West R (1989). ESU Framework: Performance Scales for English Language Examinations. Harlow: Longman. ISBN 0-582-03161-3.
- Louis Garnade and his team at the English Book Centre, Oxford (details on page 159) for their characteristic generosity in allowing us access to their database of published Business English books for Checklist 2.

Although every effort has been made to trace and contact copyright holders before publication, this has not always been possible. If notified, the publisher will be pleased to rectify any errors or omissions at the earliest opportunity. Finally, especial thanks to all the partners, trainers and administrative staff at York Associates to whom this book is dedicated and without whom it would not have been possible. Many of the ideas and examples in this book derive from discussions which have taken place, and materials which have been developed over a number of years and which would be impossible to acknowledge individually. The author and publisher therefore acknowledge, with gratitude, a general debt to the whole team.

INTRODUCTION

Teaching Business English brings together under one umbrella a range of disparate disciplines. In fact, it would be difficult to find three more different bedfellows. So, let's start in lighter vein with a fistful of quotations from those who, through their own opinions, have captured the diversity of what we, as Business English teachers, try to unite.

1 TEACHING

Housework is a breeze. Cooking is a pleasant diversion. Putting up a retaining wall is a lark. But teaching is like climbing a mountain.
Fawn M. Brodie (1915-81), U.S. biographer.
Quoted in Los Angeles Times Home Magazine (20 Feb. 1977).

It is the supreme art of the teacher to awaken joy in creative expression and knowledge.
Albert Einstein (1879-1955), German-born U.S. physicist.
Motto for the astronomy building of Junior College, Pasadena, California.

Everybody who is incapable of learning has taken to teaching.
Oscar Wilde (1854-1900), Anglo-Irish playwright, author.
Vivian, in *The Decay of Lying* (published in Intentions, 1891).

He who can, does. He who cannot, teaches.
George Bernard Shaw (1856-1950), Anglo-Irish playwright, critic.
Man and Superman, "Maxims for Revolutionists: Education" (1903).

2 BUSINESS AND COMMERCE

International business may conduct its operations with scraps of paper, but the ink it uses is human blood.
Eric Ambler (b. 1909), British novelist. Marukakis in *A Coffin for Dimitrios*, ch. 5 (1939).

Business? it's quite simple: it's other people's money.
Alexandre Dumas (1824-95), French dramatist. Giraud, in *La Question d'Argent*, act 2, sc. 7.

When you are skinning your customers you should leave some skin on to grow again so that you can skin them again.
Nikita Khrushchev (1894-1971), Soviet premier.
Quoted in *The Observer* (London, 28 May 1961), offering advice to British business people.

Deals are my art form. Other people paint beautifully on canvas or write wonderful poetry. I like making deals, preferably big deals. That's how I get my kicks.
Donald Trump (b. 1946), U.S. businessman.
The Art of the Deal, ch. 1 (1987, written with Tony Schwartz).

Being good in business is the most fascinating kind of art... Making money is art and working is art and good business is the best art.
Andy Warhol (1928-87), U.S. Pop artist. From A to B and Back Again, ch. 6 (1975).

It is very vulgar to talk about one's business. Only people like stockbrokers do that, and then merely at dinner parties.
Oscar Wilde (1854-1900), Anglo-Irish playwright, author.
Algernon, in The Importance of Being Earnest, act 3.

3 ENGLISH

My God! The English language is a form of communication! Conversation isn't just crossfire where you shoot and get shot at! Where you've got to duck for your life and aim to kill! Words aren't only bombs and bullets - no, they're little gifts, containing meanings!
Philip Roth (b. 1933), U.S. author. Portnoy's Complaint, "The Most Prevalent Form of Degradation in Erotic Life" (1967).

The English language is nobody's special property. It is the property of the imagination: it is the property of the language itself.
Derek Walcott (b. 1930), West Indian poet, playwright. Interview in Writers at Work (Eighth Series, ed. George Plimpton, 1988).

Business English is not a subject of study with a solid base. It is an evolving practice which appears in many guises around the world and which takes a variety of forms according to local conditions and requirements. Business English arises from two expediencies: the need for a means of communication between those wishing to do business internationally; and the language used for this communication – English. So, the needs of international business have spawned a teaching cadre dedicated to providing instruction in Business English.

This book attempts to bring together some of the current practices of teaching business English, though it would be impossible to collect them all. It also tries to introduce some unifying principles under which all the various forms of Business English can happily co-exist, though the author freely admits that there could be other, hitherto undiscovered, varieties which may not fit the mould. Through this exercise, I hope that I can help these three bedfellows further evolve their relationship and benefit all concerned.

Nick Brieger
York, Spring 1997

PART ONE

BACKGROUND ISSUES IN BUSINESS AND BUSINESS ENGLISH

1 Introduction to Business English

The Scope of Teaching Business English

English language teaching has gone through a radical shift of emphasis in the last twenty years, beginning with the communicative revolution of the mid-1970s. And Business English, which appeared on the ELT stage as a course programme and learning objective in the late seventies, has been shaped by a range of influences from both the ELT and the non-ELT world. Its course content reflects the diverse needs of varied learner groups – from pre-service students to in-service professionals; and its pedagogic approaches have been influenced by the learning experiences of its learners – from broadly-based general education to specifically-designed management training. So, the teaching of Business English has received noticeable contributions from:

- ELT methodologies which teach language knowledge and language skills in a range of business contexts through communicative activities
- communication training which develops the effectiveness of the total communication process by looking at the message in terms of its form and delivery
- management disciplines which provide professional content on key areas.

In short, the teaching of Business English brings together three areas:
1. teaching – the pedagogic skills involved in running training programmes
2. English – knowledge of the language and, latterly, an understanding of the role of communication in professional situations
3. business – familiarity with the key issues facing specific learners or learner groups.

Each of these areas is evolving in its own way. New teaching approaches bring in training ideas such as facilitation and moderation; language change introduces new forms; communication adapts to evolving behavioural and technological standards; and business both initiates and responds to changing practices. All in all, the menu provides a rich mix, a starting point for exploring the scope of Business English and the range of skills needed by the Business English teacher. And for any practitioner, the challenge is in the dynamic mix between:

- each teacher's own personal and humanistic approach to teaching
- the knowledge to be acquired by the learners
- the skills to be developed by the learners.

So Business English is very much a mongrel. Course content reflects the needs of its users; course delivery the personal style of its practitioners.

THE OBJECTIVES OF BUSINESS ENGLISH LEARNING AND TEACHING: ACCURACY, FLUENCY AND EFFECTIVENESS

The recent history of ELT can be divided into two periods – the pre-communicative era and the post-communicative era. Pre-1975, the emphasis of most language teaching was on developing knowledge of the language forms in terms of grammar and vocabulary. Identified through linguistic analysis, these elements were subsequently organised into teaching programmes and course materials. Students learned *about* the language rather than *how to* use it. The communicative revolution of the mid-70s clearly established fluency as the prime objective of language teaching and language training. Out went language drills; in came pair work and small group communicative activities. In the early years of the communicative revolution, accuracy was sacrificed in favour of fluency. The battle cry was 'Get the students to talk at all costs'. One could be forgiven for thinking that the 'accuracy versus fluency debate' would remain centre-stage. Yet in ESP (English for Specific Purposes), another dimension was identified, namely effectiveness, making it into a three-cornered contest. In the red corner we have accuracy, claiming that without the correct use of language forms, the results will be flawed. In the blue corner we have fluency, claiming that if you can speak, somehow you will be able to get your message over. And in the green corner we have effectiveness, claiming that it is the total performance (linguistic and non-linguistic) which determines the success or failure of communication.

The 'fluency versus effectiveness versus accuracy' debate deserves a little more attention since, in my book, they are separate areas. My reasoning goes as follows:

Firstly, all normal native speakers are fluent in their mother tongue; however, they are not all effective communicators. Therefore fluency, the objective of communicative language teaching, will not necessarily lead to effectiveness. Similarly, amongst non-native speakers, some rank fairly highly on the fluency scale, yet considerably lower on the effectiveness scale. Therefore, fluency does not equal effectiveness.

Secondly, all educated native speakers can form correct sentences in their mother tongue in terms of grammar and vocabulary. Yet this linguistic accuracy does not automatically lead to effectiveness in communication. The same is true of non-native speakers. I have taught many students who have had an excellent knowledge of linguistic forms, but who would not be considered as effective communicators. On the other hand, there are those 'natural communicators', who break the language rules, yet transmit convincing and effective messages. Therefore, accuracy does not equal effectiveness.

My conclusion is that we have three different (yet related) elements or skills: accuracy, fluency and effectiveness, as shown in the diagram which follows. And it is important that we decide which one (or two or three) our particular training course shall concentrate on.

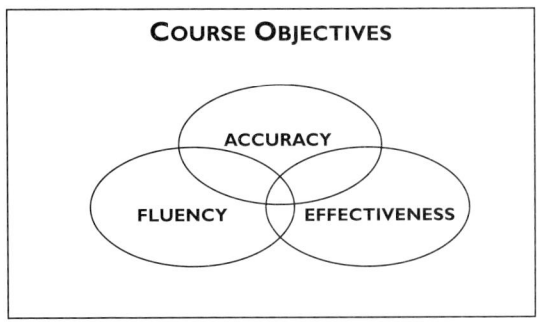

COURSE OBJECTIVES

- ACCURACY
- FLUENCY
- EFFECTIVENESS

THE SCOPE OF BUSINESS ENGLISH

In the previous section we examined the range of objectives of a Business English programme. It might be considered unconventional to look at the why before the what, but this approach highlights the need to keep the focus clearly on learners and their reasons for embarking on a programme of instruction.

Corresponding with learner objectives, we have two major elements as the building blocks for course design and a constellation of minor forces. Language knowledge reflects the formal aspects of grammar, vocabulary and the sound system. In communication we activate this knowledge to transmit messages through different channels, for example presentations, meetings, telephoning or in written documents, such as correspondence or reports. Language knowledge reflects what one knows of the language; communication skills what one knows how to do with the language. Together they are a powerful instrument in assessing overall competence.

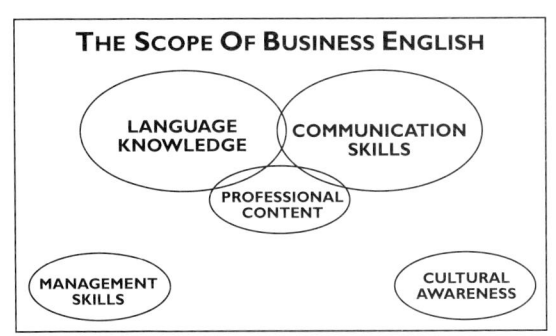

THE SCOPE OF BUSINESS ENGLISH

- LANGUAGE KNOWLEDGE
- COMMUNICATION SKILLS
- PROFESSIONAL CONTENT
- MANAGEMENT SKILLS
- CULTURAL AWARENESS

The legitimate scope of our pedagogic activities as Business English trainers is to design and deliver courses which aim to increase *language knowledge* and to develop *communication skills*.

However, what makes Business English trainers different from General English trainers is partly related to language and partly to communication.
- The *language* to be introduced and practised in the Business English classroom reflects the professional background of the learner(s).
- The channels of *communication* to be developed and practised reflect the professional world of presentations, meetings and telephoning rather than general communication in discussion.

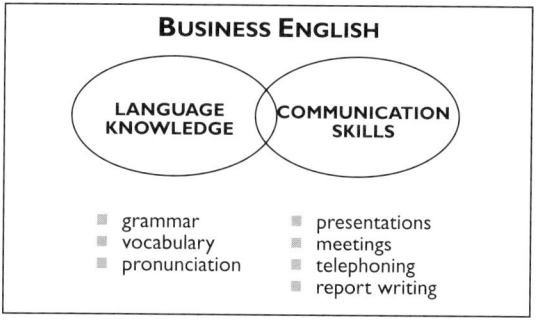

BUSINESS ENGLISH

LANGUAGE KNOWLEDGE
- grammar
- vocabulary
- pronunciation

COMMUNICATION SKILLS
- presentations
- meetings
- telephoning
- report writing

Thus, Business English draws on general English for some of its contents, while adding others which are specific to business.

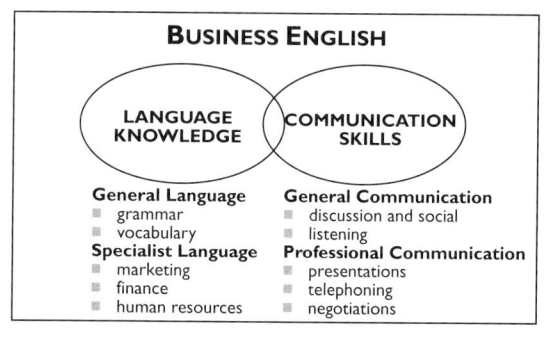

BUSINESS ENGLISH

LANGUAGE KNOWLEDGE

General Language
- grammar
- vocabulary

Specialist Language
- marketing
- finance
- human resources

COMMUNICATION SKILLS

General Communication
- discussion and social
- listening

Professional Communication
- presentations
- telephoning
- negotiations

So, while language and communication are central, the contexts of Business English are different from the contexts of General English. These contexts are reflected by the constellation of smaller ovals in the diagram on the previous page.

1 Professional Content provides a range of settings or themes related to professional functions, such as marketing or finance, or to business sectors, such as banking or pharmaceuticals. Both General English and Business English need contexts for developing language knowledge and communication skills. General English uses topics or themes; Business English takes professional content. In both cases the setting is the activation vehicle not the learning end. In other words, the use of a theme such as 'leisure activities' in the General English classroom is not to make the students experts in leisure;

similarly, when dealing with marketing issues, the Business English teacher is not aiming to teach about marketing. Providing training in professional content is the role of a management consultant, not a language trainer. Nevertheless, there is a need for the Business English teacher to know something about professional content, and this is discussed more fully in Chapter 2 – Dealing with Professional Content.

2 Management skills (see Chapter 5). Managers manage. A marketing manager manages marketing; and a production manager manages production. Although we can define the content of marketing and production, the precise activities of management are less clearly prescribed. The history of management shows that different periods have focused on different skills. Yet in the changing web of management activities, four areas stand out through time:
- planning
- leading
- organising
- controlling

A glance at the preoccupations of today's managers shows that two areas are considered the key to successful management:
- leadership in order to inspire and motivate colleagues and subordinates
- team building in order to harness the synergies of individuals brought together from different disciplines and with different specialisations.

And at the heart of both effective leadership and team building is communication.

3 Cultural awareness. Culture (see Chapter 6) refers to the values shared by a group of people. While culture has traditionally been viewed and analysed at the national level, other groups clearly share beliefs, behaviours and other traits. A set of shared values can be seen at the level of the:
- company
- department
- team

Shared values are an important factor in enhancing the togetherness of the members, thereby improving their performance.

At the end of the twentieth century, as national borders crumble in the wake of increased global business, those companies which have established a firm basis of values and principles seem better equipped to provide a secure framework for their employees and an environment in which they can flourish.

And at the heart of each entity with a strong positive culture is open and effective communication.

The York Associates Teaching Business English Handbook

THE ESP FAMILY			
COURSE TYPE	DRIVER 1	DRIVER 2	DRIVER 3
SOFT ESP	LANGUAGE	CONTENT	
COMMUNICATION SKILLS	COMMUNICATION	CONTENT	
HARD ESP	CONTENT	LANGUAGE OR COMMUNICATION	LANGUAGE OR COMMUNICATION

THE ESP FAMILY

ESP courses can be roughly divided into three main categories, depending on their structure and goals.

This table shows three members of the ESP family. Each can be considered a type of ESP course. The table goes on to show the organisational principles around which each course type is structured. I have divided these organisational principles into primary, secondary and tertiary to show their relative weight in the course design. Let's start with **soft ESP** courses.

These are courses where the primary structure of the course materials is linguistic. In other words, a glance at the contents page of a soft ESP book such as *Early Business Contacts* will show the traditional linguistic categories (grammatical, functional and lexical). So what differentiates it from a general English course? Content. However, the 'specialist' content, be it business, technical or legal, is an 'add on' to give the materials a flavour of the specific area. In other words, they are a credible teaching vehicle, but not authentic in terms of content or context. They are good for developing language knowledge and communicative fluency; they are less good at developing effectiveness in communication.

Our second member is the **communication skills** course. Here the emphasis is on effective transmission of a message. Key areas addressed in this type of programme or materials are: What is the best *medium* to use? Should it be written or face-to-face; in a presentation or through a meeting? How can the message be best *structured*? Should it be logically or chronologically; from general to specific or vice versa? And how can the message be best *delivered*? In a formal or informal style; with questions during or after the information? Here the emphasis is on developing communication techniques (in contrast to communicative fluency). As with soft ESP courses, content is not a primary focus, although it may be provided as an adjunct in order to contextualise the course within the students' professional area, e.g. effective presentations for marketing personnel or effective negotiations for finance managers. These communication skills courses are clearly valuable for communication effectiveness; they are less good at developing language accuracy or communicative fluency.

Our third member is the **hard ESP** course. Here the driving force, in organisational terms, is the learner's specialist area and the key questions which he or she needs to deal with. Below are two examples, the first from marketing and the second from personnel.

Marketing	
Marketing	**Distribution channels**
The market environment	Wholesaling and retailing
Buyer behaviour	**Promotion**
Market segmentation: targeting and positioning	Communication and advertising
	Personal selling
Products	**International marketing**
Product type and mix decisions	Entering foreign markets
Product development decisions	Global versus local marketing
Pricing	
Pricing strategies	
Placing	

Personnel	
Job analysis	**Training and development**
Job description	Identifying training needs
Person specification	On-the-job training methods
Planning and recruiting	**Compensation, incentives and benefits**
Personnel requirements	Pay
Recruiting job candidates	Incentives and benefits
Job advertising	
Selection and interviewing	**Appraisal and career management**
Selection methods	Appraisal
Interview structure and conduct	Career planning and management

CONCLUSION

The hallmark of ESP courses is their specificity in relation to student needs. But what exactly do we as trainers mean by specific? And is our perception the same as our students'? I believe that we can do a lot to explain to our learners the precise range of course choices that are available to them. In this first chapter I presented three ESP course types. Of course, as with any customised product, we don't need to limit ourselves to these hybrids. We can offer, for example, a soft-core course with some hard segments; in other words a language course with some work on key content areas. Or a communication skills course with some remedial soft segments; in other words a communication skills course with feedback on problematic language areas. Finally, ESP means that learners can exercise choice and one of our tasks, as trainers, is to present the choice and help them decide how they want their course prepared.

> **DISCUSSION**
> 1 Which of the three (language, communication or content) dominate your teaching?
> 2 What role do cross-cultural aspects have in your teaching?
> 3 Do you think Business English teachers need to concern themselves with management skills?

TEACHERS OF BUSINESS ENGLISH

As we have seen, Business English is a multi-faceted subject. As would be expected, those who work as teachers in this profession can be found in a range of institutional and non-institutional environments. Just as there is no single Business English, there is no single profile of a Business English teacher. The profile is fashioned by the characteristics of the working environment and its view of Business English, as well as by the demands of the learners. However, it is important to remember that the majority of teachers, as in other branches of ELT, are non-native speakers, largely trained within the local community.

Here are some typical teaching positions/jobs in the Business English world:

1 Freelance. Freelance is to teaching what consultants are to business. In other words, the freelancer provides his/her specialist expertise in designing and/or running courses for an organisation. The organisation may be a company, a school or a training organisation. By the nature of employment regulations, those who choose the freelance path will typically work with (as opposed to for) a number of different organisations. This flexibility can be attractive both for the freelancer and the organisation:

- at times of high demand, freelancers can, in theory, negotiate their own contracts and fees
- a range of teaching environments can help to increase knowledge and skills by providing opportunities for running courses for learners from different backgrounds
- as independent workers, freelancers can choose when, where and how much to work.

However, when work is scarce, the contrary is true and the freelancer may find the demands of searching for work less attractive. In addition, freelance work can be rather solitary without the backup and companionship of workplace colleagues.

Teachers in the following categories may be freelance, permanent full- or part-time or a combination of these.

2 In-company. Some companies, both large and small, have their own language training department. The courses offered in-company can include both general English and Business English programmes.

Teachers who spend a lot of their time working for one company or in one sector are likely to build up an in-depth knowledge of activities within that area as well as an insight into corporate life. This can provide an additional dimension to the teacher's job, satisfying a need for continued professional development on two fronts – pedagogic and corporate. This can be especially motivating where the teacher is given an opportunity or is encouraged to learn about the company. In fact, it is not unknown for in-company teachers to move into management positions, especially in the field of Human Resources. A second result of this increased specialisation is that in-company teachers can make themselves indispensable in developing hard ESP programmes, where content is an essential element in the course design.

Of course, narrow specialisation can also be limiting – both personally and professionally – and teachers who have spent a long time in one setting may find it difficult to adapt to the demands of a different working environment – a dilemma faced by many professionals as companies restructure and downsize to better face business challenges.

3 Language schools. Language schools typically offer general English programmes for students from different backgrounds, grouped according to language ability. However, many language schools have added Business English to their portfolio of subjects in order to target a wider range of students. Business English may be offered on the school's menu in one or more of the following ways:

- intensive group programmes throughout the year
- intensive individual programmes throughout the year
- as an optional part of a general English programme for a set number of sessions per week.

In addition, many schools will offer individual (one-to-one) classes on an hourly basis, sometimes as an add-on to a group programme (general or Business English).

For the Business English teacher, the language school environment can provide a good mix of opportunities and challenges as courses generally draw their participants from a variety of backgrounds (national and professional) with a range of different needs and objectives.

4 Academic institutions. The teaching of Business English is not restricted to in-service professionals. More and more universities and colleges are launching programmes for their pre-service students in order to prepare them for the professional world in terms of language and business. Typically, a Business English programme will be offered to students following a degree course in Business Management, Economics or a related subject. This means that teachers who previously provided general English teaching are being required to offer Business English. However, the scope of Business English varies enormously between institutions and, in the absence of agreed standards, syllabuses and programmes display very different features, content and objectives.

5 Training organisations. Training organisations resemble language schools in that they are part of the teaching world; they differ in that they typically specialise in offering customised or specialised programmes for in- and pre-service professionals. The focus of these programmes covers a wide spectrum of professional training – including technical, management and communication training. And it is within this arena that a number of organisations have sprung up specialising in Business English. Teachers working in this environment, normally called trainers, are likely to be working on short programmes with students, often called course participants, from a range of different companies. This, therefore, provides a challenging and varied environment.

> **DISCUSSION**
> 1 What sort of job do you aspire to and why?
> 2 What are the advantages and disadvantages of in-company teaching?

LEARNERS OF BUSINESS ENGLISH

Learners of Business English come from a range of different backgrounds so that trying to categorise them professionally requires a good deal of background knowledge about business. However, we can start with a basic division of learners into:
- pre-service, i.e. those with no business experience
- in-service, i.e. those already in business.

Besides differences in knowledge of management practices (and perhaps of underlying management concepts, too), this distinction is likely to translate into variations in terms of language knowledge and communication skills. These may, in turn, have implications for course objectives, design and delivery. Based on the scope of Business English, we may find the following features when contrasting pre-service and in-service learners.

PRE-SERVICE VS IN-SERVICE LEARNERS

LANGUAGE KNOWLEDGE / COMMUNICATION SKILLS

General Language
May have some knowledge of…
- grammar
- vocabulary

Specialist Language
In-service likely to have more extensive knowledge.

General Communication
May have equal skills in…
- discussion and social
- listening

Professional Communication
In-service likely to have more developed skills.

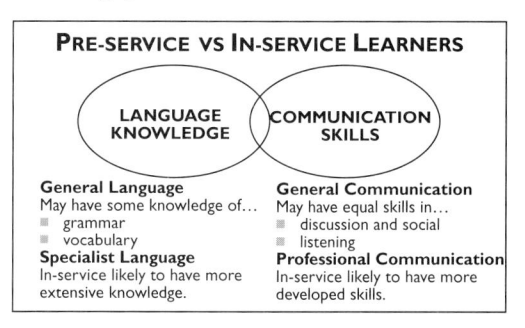

However, what all learners share is a recognition of the utility of English. This is neither an academic pastime nor a remote subject of study. English is the international language that all learners are likely to have a need for – in terms of listening, speaking, reading or writing or any combination of these skills. Thus for the pre-service student, language learning is seen as acquiring a practical tool even though there may be no immediate need for it. And while language students have chosen to study a language out of an interest in its literature, its culture or simply its linguistic forms, students from other disciplines (management, sciences, architecture, engineering, etc.) may have language study thrust upon them as part of their programme in order to prepare them for future contacts beyond their national borders.

For the in-service professional, either already following or preparing for an international career, an interest in developing competence (accuracy, fluency, effectiveness) in English may take on greater immediacy. It may be the gateway to promotion, the requirement for an international posting or the means to success in next week's presentation to management. The motivations for acquiring improved competence are extremely varied and the objectives of individuals on Business English group courses may be difficult to reconcile.

Despite these individual differences in background and objectives, it is possible to fit 'developing language competence' into a wider framework of needs for the individual with current or future needs for international communication.

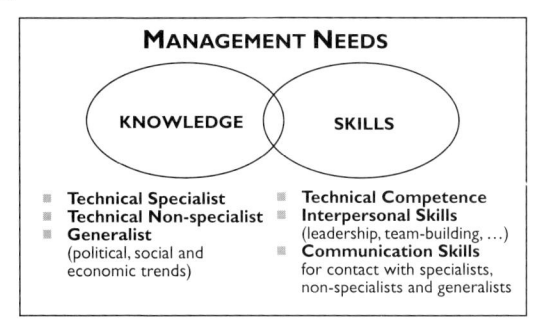

MANAGEMENT NEEDS

KNOWLEDGE / SKILLS

- Technical Specialist
- Technical Non-specialist
- Generalist
  (political, social and economic trends)

- Technical Competence
- Interpersonal Skills
  (leadership, team-building, ...)
- Communication Skills
  for contact with specialists, non-specialists and generalists

Just as we have summarised 'language competence' in terms of knowledge and skills, we can view 'management needs' in the same terms, though with different contents. Firstly, well-rounded international managers need to be technical specialists with detailed knowledge of their management areas. Secondly, with the increasing trend towards team-working, they need to understand (though not in-depth) other areas of management in order to be able to participate in cross-disciplinary teams. And thirdly, in terms of knowledge, the well-balanced manager needs to be aware of general trends in society at large in the realms of politics, economics and social trends. This is a summary of the armoury of knowledge. Using this knowledge base effectively is what gives managers their edge and enables them to operate successfully. So this knowledge needs to be complemented by a repertoire of skills.

Firstly, the manager needs to be able to translate the specialist technical knowledge into technical competence in order to achieve results. Knowing about management (and specialist areas such as marketing, production, personnel, etc.) is the knowledge base; knowing how to manage effectively is the corresponding skill. So, for every area of specialist knowledge there is a matching area of technical skill. Of course, having the knowledge does not necessarily mean having the skill. And that is precisely why we need two sides to the competence model – knowledge and skills. Yet being able to do the job involves more than just technical skill. Today's managers do not work in isolation. They are at once leaders and team players, sharing with colleagues, persuading superiors, inspiring and motivating subordinates. Playing a lead role as well as a team role requires interpersonal skills so that managers can achieve their objectives as well as enabling others to achieve theirs. By harnessing the talents of a group of individuals, managers ensure that group contributions are greater than the sum of individual efforts – the synergy effect. The final area of expertise for competent management is the raft of communication skills that enable messages of all sorts to be transmitted effectively. In addition to the professional communication skills themselves (listed in Chapter 1 under the Scope of Business English), we can identify three contexts for communication: between specialists, between specialist and non-specialist and between generalists. The first places the manager in a communicative setting where all the participants share the same technical knowledge. The second is a context where the specialist needs to share his/her knowledge with others who are not specialists in the area under consideration. This would be typical of a project team made up of managers from different disciplines. The third context is removed from day-to-day management concerns and focuses on the type of communication required outside the strict business setting – information exchange and discussions about social, economic or other topical matters. All of these contexts of communication require different skills, as well as different language. (For more on the language aspect, see Chapter 3.)

In conclusion, it is not easy to define the Business English learner. In fact, it is perhaps precisely because they come with such different track records and such a range of needs and expectations that Business English itself is difficult to pin down. In short, there are as many approaches to Business English as there are course types. Our task, as trainers, is to put together programmes which respond to the needs and expectations of our diverse learners.

> ### DISCUSSION
> 1 Which would you prefer to teach: pre-service or in-service students? What would be the main differences?
> 2 What do you consider the most important attributes of a good manager?

BUSINESS ENGLISH VERSUS GENERAL ENGLISH: SOME CONTRASTS

In the introductory section, we looked at a number of key issues in the teaching and learning of Business English. There are other factors which we will look at in part 2 of the book, when we consider pedagogic and classroom issues. However, at this point, I'd like to offer the following summary chart of some key contrasts between the Business English and the General English classroom.

Business English		General English
	Programmes	
Focus on developing: ■ accuracy ■ fluency ■ effectiveness *Focus on developing:* ■ general and specialist language knowledge ■ general and professional communication skills		*Focus on developing:* ■ accuracy ■ fluency *Focus on developing:* ■ general language knowledge ■ general communication skills
	Learners	
Drawn from: ■ Pre-service ■ In-service		*Drawn from:* ■ Pre-service ■ In-service
	Trainers	
Need the following mix of knowledge and skills: ■ ELT methodology ■ communication skills training ■ knowledge of business content		*Need the following mix of knowledge and skills:* ■ ELT methodology
	Methodology	
Based on: ■ communicative ELT methodology ■ communication skills training		*Based on:* ■ communicative ELT methodology

> **DISCUSSION**
> 1 How much do you think ESP can learn from General English methodology?
> 2 What do you think General English teachers can learn from ESP teachers?

2 Dealing with Professional Content

Content – the contentious issue

The role of professional content in Business English training is unquestionably the single most controversial issue in the mix of course design. On the one side there are those teachers who clearly see their classroom focus in terms of teaching language. Business is not their domain and professional activities are a slender backdrop against which language knowledge is developed. The contrary view is expressed by many training organisations and in-company training departments. The former are likely to have built up a strong relationship with key clients and can therefore provide trainers with sufficient expertise in a range of professional areas to be able to provide a flexible mix of language and content. The latter, whose trainers have worked extensively within the organisation, are likely to have developed in-depth knowledge of the organisation's activities.

It is not my purpose here to enter into the debate about the role of content, but simply to point out the differences in philosophy and approach which exist. Business English is not a clearly-defined subject of instruction but rather an umbrella term for a range of programmes driven by customer needs. What is clear, though, is that language teachers are not content specialists. They cannot be expected to provide management training within the guise of language teaching. However, the limits of their knowledge are vague and are fashioned by usage rather than rules. The in-company language teacher is likely to have developed more knowledge relating to a specialist area, i.e. the company's activities, than the language school Business English teacher who runs courses for learners from different professional backgrounds. This is not to demean the latter or to glorify the former.

The following diagram charts the roles that Business English teachers may be requested to perform in the classroom. The use of a cline does highlight differences in status and, with it, pay. Language teachers are highly valued but often low paid, at least in comparison with management consultants. And, generally speaking, the greater a teacher's specialisation or, at least, range of professional expertise, the greater the salary or fee that he/she can command. Having said that, the boundaries between the different points on the cline, as with many aspects of Business English, are imprecise. In addition, one teacher may occupy more than one position, depending on who the client or learner is.

At one end of the spectrum is the role of language teacher/language trainer, representing courses which focus principally on language development within a framework of business-oriented vocabulary. At the other end are

THE TEACHING/TRAINING CLINE

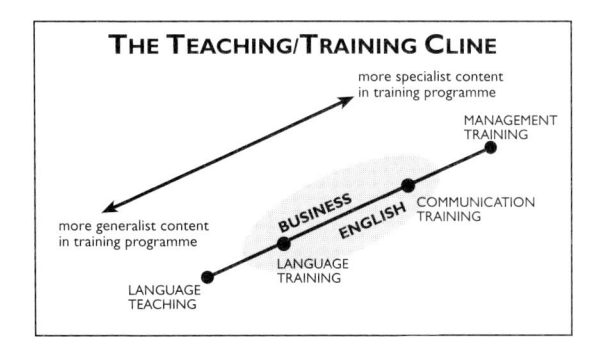

```
                                    more specialist content
                                    in training programme
                                                        MANAGEMENT
                                                        TRAINING
                                          BUSINESS  COMMUNICATION
   more generalist content                ENGLISH   TRAINING
   in training programme
                                         LANGUAGE
                                         TRAINING
              LANGUAGE
              TEACHING
```

programmes where content, language and communication are combined in order to develop the learner's language knowledge and communication skills. However, the trainer is not a content specialist aiming to teach the management content, but rather a knowledgeable generalist able to tap into the learner's expertise and use it as a resource in the development of the course. As an example, let's take a course for finance managers who need to develop their language knowledge and communication skills for handling communication and exchanges on professional matters. These professional matters may include financial reports such as balance sheets and profit and loss statements. The type of Business English course prepared for such a group may focus on one or more of the following areas, depending on the needs of the participants and the skills of the trainer:

- developing language knowledge within the context of general business and financial topics
- developing professional communication skills within the context of general business and financial topics
- developing specialist language knowledge within the context of specialist financial topics
- developing professional communication skills within the context of specialist financial topics.

Clearly the Business English teacher with little or no experience of the financial world would have difficulty designing a course which dealt with specialist financial topics. This is not to demean the general Business English teacher, but simply to point out the realities lying beneath the umbrella of Business English.

As we have seen, the role of content is a controversial issue. As long as Business English remains an umbrella for a wide range of course types, it is unlikely that the position of content will be unambiguously defined. However, for both the existing and the future teacher, the key issues for reflection are:

- personal / professional targets along the cline
- methods for achieving them.

> **DISCUSSION**
> 1 Look again at the diagram in this section and plot your position(s) on it for the classroom roles that you are expected to perform.
> 2 Are there content-based areas where you:
>   - have special knowledge or expertise?
>   - would like to develop your knowledge?

ORGANISATIONS IN BUSINESS

The world of business encompasses many areas and activities. Getting an idea of the range is a daunting task even for the experienced business professional. Fortunately, the typical middle manager stays broadly within his/her specialism. The wide-ranging Business English teacher may, however, need to train participants from different areas on a regular basis. In the absence of a management background, how can Business English teachers make sense of the corporate world and its workforce?

A useful starting point is to look at:
- the types of business organisations (legal entities)
- management and management activities
- the key functions in a business organisation by departmental activities
- the main sectors in which businesses operate.

These are the areas covered in the remainder of this chapter, starting with organisation.

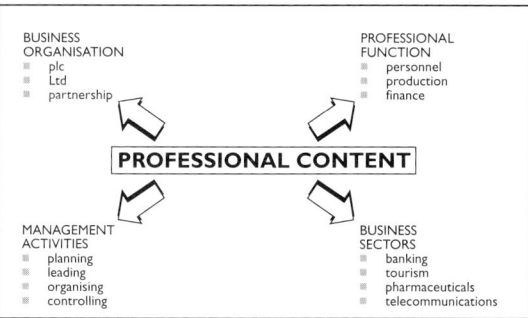

```
BUSINESS                          PROFESSIONAL
ORGANISATION                      FUNCTION
  ■ plc                             ■ personnel
  ■ Ltd                             ■ production
  ■ partnership                     ■ finance

              PROFESSIONAL CONTENT

MANAGEMENT                        BUSINESS
ACTIVITIES                        SECTORS
  ■ planning                        ■ banking
  ■ leading                         ■ tourism
  ■ organising                      ■ pharmaceuticals
  ■ controlling                     ■ telecommunications
```

The following analysis is based on Anglo-Saxon company models and Euro-American company organisations.

Public Limited Company (plc or PLC). A plc is a legal entity formed for the purpose of conducting business. It is owned by its shareholders, who may be private individuals or corporate institutions. The company issues shares in order to raise capital. Investors subscribe to shares in order to benefit from the financial success of the company through dividends paid out from profits.

However, if a company performs badly, the liability of the shareholders for the company's losses is limited to the money paid for the shares. Shares are traded on one or more stock exchanges. Plc's are typically large international or multinational corporations. Their activities have a high degree of transparency and are closely monitored by business analysts who report in the business press about successes, failures, take-overs, mergers and restructuring.

Private Limited Company (Ltd.). A limited company is also a legal entity. It is owned by its shareholders, who are typically private individuals. When the company makes a profit, the shareholders expect to receive a dividend from the profits declared. However, if the company makes a loss, the liability of the shareholders is limited to the money paid for the shares. Limited companies cannot sell shares to or raise capital from the general public. Limited companies are typically smaller than plc's.

Associated Company. A company over which another company has substantial influence; for example it owns between 20 per cent and 50 per cent of its shares.

Holding Company. A company that owns another company or other companies and which is sometimes referred to as the parent company. (Most public companies operate through a number of companies controlled by the group's holding company.)

Subsidiary Company. A company controlled by a holding company, usually because the holding company owns (or indirectly owns through another subsidiary) more than 50 per cent of the subsidiary company's shares.

Partnership. A partnership is an association of two or more persons who have agreed by legal contract to combine their efforts, property, and skill, or some or all of them, to engage in lawful business activities. The partners of an organisation share profits and losses between them and therefore have unlimited liability for the debts of the company.

Sole Trader. A sole trader is a person who conducts business on his or her own behalf with full entitlement to all profits made but with full liability for all losses incurred.

THE EVOLUTION OF MANAGEMENT

Although not every business English student is a manager in the hierarchical sense, all will be involved with the management of resources – time, money, people and materials. Therefore an understanding of underlying management principles will help Business English teachers to better orientate their courses to meet the needs of their students.

Mecson, Albert and Khedouri define management as 'the process of planning, organising, leading and controlling the work of organisation members and of using all available organisational resources to reach stated organisational goals'.

A rather more accessible definition, or explanation, appears in Mary Parker Follett's 1918 book, *The New State*, in which she observes that management is 'the art of getting things done through people'. This highlights the fact that managers arrange for others to fulfil the required organisational tasks rather than performing the tasks themselves.

Together, these two definitions highlight the ambiguity between management as a scientific process and a personal skill. In fact, more detailed reading in management theory and management principles will show that while it is relatively easy to agree on what management is about, it is rather more difficult to identify the precise activities that will achieve the organisation's goals. This is hardly surprising as there is no single set of management practices that are held to be universally constant. They change with the changing organisational structures that they are meant to serve. This does not in any way reduce management to a maverick activity – something that the gifted few are born with – but rather focuses on its proactive and reactive features, responding to the business environment.

Over the years these changes in business environment have led to, or perhaps given rise to, a number of different management schools.

SCIENTIFIC MANAGEMENT

This management approach, formulated by Frederick W. Taylor (1856-1915) and others between 1890 and 1930, sought to determine scientifically the best methods for performing any task, and for selecting, training, and motivating workers. It arose in part out of a need to increase productivity at the beginning of the twentieth century, in heavy industries such as steel. According to Taylor (and beliefs about human nature at the time), people were rational beings, motivated primarily by material gain. A combination of the ideal working environment and the appropriate reward would create the efficiencies required to increase productivity. Taylor's approach was through a detailed analysis of the operations required by any job and the subsequent allocation of the precise human and material resources needed to fulfil it. This would lead to higher productivity – the key to commercial success. In return for higher productivity, workers would be rewarded with higher wages.

The four basic principles upon which Taylor based his ideas were:
1. the development of a true science of management, so that the best method for performing each task could be determined
2. the scientific selection of the workers, so that each worker would be

given responsibility for the task for which he or she was best suited
3 the scientific education and development of the worker
4 intimate, friendly co-operation between management and labour.

The legacy of Taylor's approach can be seen in the efficiency of modern conveyor belt production. However, the supporters of scientific management, in their quest for ideal systems, overlooked the need for other motivating factors besides money. In fact, it soon became clear that once the workers had achieved a certain level of affluence, they were much more likely to withdraw their labour over job conditions than over salary demands. Thus the rational approach to human nature, where money is the prime motivator, became an increasingly inappropriate basis for a management model.

CLASSICAL ORGANISATION THEORY

The recognition of the importance of the human factor in the working environment led to the Classical Organisation Theory. While Taylor had concentrated his efforts on increasing productivity, proponents of classical organisation focused on managerial behaviour. Henri Fayol (1841-1925), generally acknowledged as the founder of this school, believed that 'with scientific forecasting and proper methods of management, satisfactory results were inevitable'. He firmly believed that management was not an innate talent but rather a learned skill. The belief that managers are made, not born, was a reversal of earlier thinking.

Fayol divided business operations into six interdependent and related functional areas:
1 Technical – producing and manufacturing
2 Commercial – buying raw materials and selling finished goods
3 Financial – raising and using capital
4 Security – protecting employees and property
5 Accounting – recording and controlling financial transactions
6 Managerial – overviewing the company's activities.

In this list we can see the seeds of the departmental organisation found in many manufacturing companies today.

Superimposed on the above list was Fayol's view of what management was essentially about and the skills needed by a manager. These can be summarised as:
1 Planning – drawing up plans to enable the organisation to meet its goals
2 Organising – employing the human and material resources to implement the plans
3 Commanding – providing direction for the workers and getting them to do their jobs
4 Co-ordinating – ensuring that human and material resources are working harmoniously to achieve the desired goals
5 Controlling – monitoring all the processes to ensure they are being carried out correctly.

In this way, Fayol added managerial activities to the functional tasks. While Taylor had viewed his workforce as units of production, Fayol took account of human differences. 'We have to allow for different and changing circumstance, for human beings who are equally different and changeable, and for many other variable elements'. Fayol preferred to talk about principles of management which were flexible tools, capable of being adapted to meet the needs of changing circumstances. However, in comparison with the end of the twentieth century, organisations at that time were relatively stable and the principles formed a well-balanced yet flexible approach for managing large but simple organisational structures.

While many of Fayol's principles have stood the test of time and can be widely seen in today's management practices, organisations have changed (and are changing) regularly and dramatically. One distinct area is through work specialisation. On the one hand, increased focalisation has produced specialists with narrowly-defined areas of activity; on the other, cross-fertilisation of ideas has created cross-functional groups, where participants share specialist knowledge in order to find innovative solutions to complex challenges. A second distinct area is in the recognition of the human factor in organisations – an organisation is its people.

BEHAVIOURAL MOVEMENTS

The classical schools helped introduce people into the management equation, but failed to solve the frustrations that managers felt when people did not behave in predicted or predictable ways. Two emerging human sciences, psychology and sociology, were called upon to provide insights into human behaviour. The results were known as the human relations approach and the focus of its proponents was on how to deal more effectively with the people in the organisation by addressing social needs.

The human relations movement (from the Second World War on) has developed and improved the classical approach by highlighting three areas:
1. the functional areas where management is needed, based on Fayol's analysis
2. the organisational skills required for effective management, based again on Fayol's analysis
3. the human skills required for effective management, in other words how to manage people – not only as individuals but also as groups.

This has led to an emphasis on improving the work environment in order to increase productivity. Initiatives such as job rotation, labour-management councils and training opportunities have been employed to increase job satisfaction and worker motivation. The results show that although these factors do, in many cases, contribute to increased job satisfaction, there is no automatic correlation between improved working environment and increased worker output. When it comes to the work environment, the human condition responds variously and unpredictably. This creates problems for

Background Issues in Business and Business English

those trying to establish a scientific basis for human behaviour, for without constancy there are only variables.

Subsequent researchers have further developed this behavioural approach, continuing to stress the importance of people in their work environment. This group, known as Behavioural Scientists rather than Human Relations Theorists, believed that various forces were at work in the motivation of 'social man'. Maslow, one of the most famous of the group, showed the needs that we are motivated to fulfil or have fulfilled through a hierarchical representation.

```
        /\
       /  \
      / Self- \
     /actualisation\
    /   needs    \
   /--------------\
  /  Esteem needs  \
 /------------------\
 / Belongingness needs \
/----------------------\
/    Safety needs       \
/------------------------\
/  Physiological needs    \
/--------------------------\
```

Maslow's proposition is that an individual's lower level needs must be satisfied before higher level needs can be met. However, in our society, many lower level needs are satisfied outside work or are taken for granted in work. For example, a safe work environment is not considered a motivating factor for the average worker, where the expectation is that the employer will provide low-risk equipment and a safe workplace. Therefore, for our working environment to be motivating, it needs to satisfy those higher level needs. And it is important for superiors to recognise this when trying to motivate subordinates.

Some later researchers argue that Maslow's analysis does not take account of the complexities of human nature. They argue for 'complex man', saying that for some people, work is only a means to an end – to satisfy their lower-level needs; for others, work provides an opportunity for meeting and satisfying higher-level needs.

The Behavioural Scientists, including the Human Relations Theorists, have been very influential in forming the discipline of modern management. Their contributions have been particularly useful in fields such as:
- individual motivation
- group behaviour
- interpersonal relationships
- the importance of work to human beings.

The findings have helped managers become more sensitive and sophisticated in their dealings with colleagues and subordinates. They continue to offer insights into current management concerns such as leadership, team building, delegation and communication.

MANAGEMENT SCIENCE
The Management Scientists represents a third major movement. Born out of the need to find solutions to complex, multi-disciplinary problems, teams of specialists from different areas are teamed together to build a mathematical model to simulate the problem. This synergy, coupled with the technological power now available, has produced solutions in areas such as capital budgeting, production scheduling and inventory control. The strength of the management science approach is in pooling expertise to solve cross-functional problems; its weakness is that it has not yet found ways of integrating the insights from behavioural models. As a result, implementation of actions fails because the psychological and behavioural aspects of the workplace are not adequately considered.

CONCLUSION
These three schools of management thought have emerged over the last hundred years, each developing and reacting to its predecessor. All continue to exert an influence on management thought today and co-exist as management science continues to evolve.

> **DISCUSSION**
> In what ways is the background information in this chapter useful for:
> - understanding management?
> - understanding managers?
> - designing Business English courses?

THE DIVISION OF LABOUR

In the first part of this chapter, we looked at the legal organisation of business, which provided a starting point for understanding the structure of business entities. We then saw how management practices evolved to handle complex organisations and activities. By breaking down the work into manageable units, managers were able to exercise control; and by creating hierarchies they were able to delegate tasks to subordinates.

These practices are translated into the company hierarchy, which gives us a further insight into the organisation of the business world. The organigram (company flowchart) is traditionally a top-down representation with power flowing through levels of management, from senior management through middle management to junior / lower management.

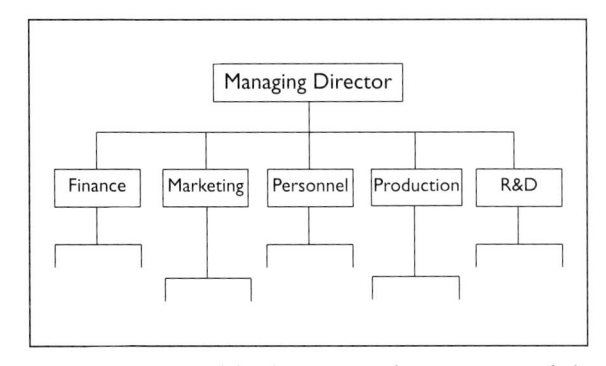

Background Issues in Business and Business English

```
                    ┌──────────────────┐
                    │ Managing Director│
                    └──────────────────┘
       ┌──────┬─────────┼─────────┬──────┐
    ┌──────┐┌────────┐┌────────┐┌──────────┐┌─────┐
    │Finance││Marketing││Personnel││Production││R&D │
    └──────┘└────────┘└────────┘└──────────┘└─────┘
```

While a company is required by law to conform to one of the entities described earlier, the company hierarchy does not follow such fixed rules. For example, in Company A, the personnel director may be part of the senior management team; in Company B the personnel function may be carried out by a middle manager in the administration department. However, there are some constants based around the core activities that companies need to carry out, to fulfil their business activities as well as their legal requirements. These constants do, in many cases, translate into departments with clearly defined titles and responsibilities. However, it is important to remember that the corporate hierarchy is not set in stone; and in recent years, many companies have sought to remove whole layers of management in order to become more responsive, less hierarchical and more efficient. (Terms for this have included restructuring, down-sizing, slimming down and have included all grades – from senior management down to the shopfloor).

There is another reason why the functional hierarchy is a useful starting point for exploring a company's activities: simplicity. Even the most complex company needs a closed-ended and transparent structure. In other words, it would be pointless to duplicate efforts by having two or more departments with identical functions; similarly, it would be impractical for one individual to have a large number of bosses to report to. Therefore, what one tends to find in an organigram is a discrete number of areas, each devoted to one key function, in a pyramidal form, with power flowing down from a senior position. Thus it is possible to get an overview of the functional structure without understanding the technicalities of the underlying responsibilities.

The following flowchart is a classical model based around the notion of a traditional company hierarchy, which serves to show the link between departments and core activities. It can also be thought of as an identification tag for the manager or director inasmuch as it shows one way of answering the question: What do you do? As work plays a formative role in our identities, the responses are likely to include:

- I'm in personnel.
- I work in the personnel department.
- I work as a personnel manager.

The York Associates Teaching Business English Handbook

All of these replies give us a link to the individual's function, position or both. And this, in turn, leads us to the company hierarchy.

- Managing Director (US: Chief Executive Officer)
- Administration
- Customer Service
- Distribution
- Finance
- Legal
- Marketing
- Personnel
- Production
- Purchasing
- Research & Development
- Sales

This organigram is a template for exploring and understanding corporate structures. It is not prescriptive. Configurations differ between similar organisations. So trainers may find themselves working with participants from these areas, but differently organised. For example, in some companies sales is part of marketing, personnel is part of administration and customer service is part of sales.

In addition, the above list is not exhaustive and trainers may find themselves working with participants from other professional areas, such as:

Design	Legal	Public Relations
Engineering	Logistics	Quality
Environment	(including distribution)	Secretarial
Health and safety	Materials management	Security
Information technology	Project management	Training

While the Managing Director is always a member of the company's senior management and sits on the Board of Directors, the status of the other senior members will be a matter of a specific organisation's practice rather than a fixed regulation. So, the heads of the above departments may be either senior managers or middle managers, depending on convention.

A brief description of each department and the key functions follows:

The Managing Director (US: Chief Executive Officer) is responsible for the day-to-day management of a company. He or she is supported in that activity by a number of departments.

The Administration Department provides ways of checking on, watching over and supporting the operations of the company. In many companies, the data processing section, which provides information and data about finance, production, sales, etc. is located within the administration department.

The Customer Service Department deals with customers before and after a sale. These services are also called pre-sales and after-sales. The department looks after customers' orders, complaints and after-sales.

The Distribution Department (or Logistics Department) looks after the flow of materials into and out of the company or factory.

The Finance Department is responsible for all aspects of a company's finance. These include forecasting, budgeting and controlling all transactions coming into and going out of the company.

The Legal Department handles areas which involve the law. These can include contract drafting and matters involving legislation and litigation.

The Marketing Department is responsible for a spread of activities which aim to inform existing and potential customers about a company's products and services, and ultimately lead to sales.

The Personnel Department is concerned with the company's people. This includes forecasting manpower needs, recruitment, selection, training and development, compensation and benefits, community links and environmental policies.

The Production (and Operations) Department is concerned with the transformation of inputs into outputs. In a manufacturing company, the production work revolves around the factory unit where the conversion of raw materials into finished products takes place. In a service company, operations is concerned with tasks related to the company's core activities e.g. typing letters, advising clients or providing training. In both cases, two central concerns are how to increase productivity and how to improve quality.

The Purchasing Department is responsible for buying goods and materials needed for the company's activities. These may be raw materials for the production process or office supplies for other departments. The objective of purchasing is 'to purchase the right quality of material, at the right time, in the right quantity, from the right source, at the right price, to be delivered as, when and where necessary'. By centralising purchasing, companies can develop relationships with suppliers to ensure quality products at competitive prices.

The Research and Development Department carries out scientific investigations which can lead to new products or services or the improvement of existing ones. R & D has been described by management guru Kotler (in his book *Marketing Management*), as 'the life blood of the company'.

The Sales Department is responsible for selling the goods or services which a company offers. A company may use various methods for selling: face-to-face using sales representatives in charge of a territory or a (number of) key account(s), or telephone sales involving regular phone calls to existing or potential customers.

KEY ISSUES IN MANAGEMENT

For the Business English teacher, it is also clearly useful to know something of the key issues that managers and their teams from different areas have to face. These concerns are partly general and partly local. The general part stems from the type of management function and the nature of the job; the local part stems from factors affecting that company in its own setting (geographical, financial, etc.). This depth of understanding will depend on a number of factors, including:
- learner expectations
- client requirements
- trainer interest.

The following lists are intended as a helpful starting point for exploring different management interests and concerns. In general, the key concerns are linked to basic business concepts. An introduction to key vocabulary related to these areas is given in Part 3.

GENERAL MANAGEMENT
The following five categories illustrate concerns for all managers:
Planning
- establishing goals and standards
- developing rules and procedures
- developing plans
- forecasting and projecting the future

Organising
- giving each member of the management team a specific task
- establishing departments
- delegating authority
- establishing channels of authority and communication
- co-ordinating the work of the management team

Staffing
- deciding what type of people should be hired
- setting performance standards
- evaluating performance

- counselling

Leading
- getting others to get the job done
- maintaining morale
- motivating subordinates

Controlling
- setting standards
- checking to compare actual performance against standards
- taking corrective action, as needed

ADMINISTRATION
Information systems
Information flow
Technology and equipment for providing information

CUSTOMER SERVICE
Satisfying customer needs so that the customer has:
- the right product (availability and quality)
- at the right place (delivery)
- at the right time (phasing)
- at an acceptable and agreed price (pricing)

Having qualified staff to handle:
- customer enquiries about product availability and product features
- customer returns for various reasons, including delivery of wrong or non-quality products
- customer complaints because of non-quality products

DISTRIBUTION
This includes the movement of goods from the manufacturer's production centre (factory) to the customer's reception centre.
Having qualified staff to manage the movement of goods
Having the right documentation to ensure the correct movement of goods
Having the means of transportation which is:
- well-maintained, in the case of own transport
- reliable, in the case of third party contractors
- economic, in both cases

Having the means of transportation to get the goods to the customer:
- at the right time
- in good condition
- at an economic price

FINANCE
Financial accounting
- recording the results of business transactions

- collecting income and paying debts
- preparing statutory financial statements

Treasury
- ensuring the company receives the best return on cash not presently used
- providing enough cash to pay debts
- foreign exchange transactions
- providing information on cash flow for reporting and budgeting

Management accounting
- recording, interpreting and analysing financial information for internal planning, control and decision-making

Systems
- planning computer strategy
- reducing complexities in the availability and flow of information
- providing database financial and non-financial information
- selecting computer equipment
- implementing computer systems

Internal audit
- examining and reporting on the effectiveness of policies, procedures and programmes
- advising on new control procedures
- examining areas of the business for improved value for money

LEGAL

Responsible for legal affairs of the company, in particular:
- contract drafting
- legislation affecting the company's activities, eg health and safety regulations
- company rules and regulations
- litigation
- selecting specialist legal advisors
- dealing with government departments
- advising internally on legal position

MARKETING

These activities are often referred to as the four (or the seven) P's:
1. Product – the goods or services to be sold
2. Price – the cost of the product
3. Promotion – means of informing people about the product or service, e.g. advertising
4. Place – the means of getting the product or service to the customer
5. Packaging – the wrapping or box for the product, but also all added-value or intangible assets
6. People – everyone involved from producer to consumer
7. Phasing – everything to do with time.

Personnel
Job analysis (determining the nature of each employee's job)
Planning manpower needs
Recruiting and selecting job candidates
Orienting and training new employees
Compensation (wages and salaries)
Providing incentives and benefits
Appraising performance
Face-to-face communication
Management development
The legal framework (equal opportunities, health and safety, labour relations)

Production
Planning operations
- costs, economies and capacity
- facilities location
- facilities layout

Organising operations
- job design and work measurement
- project management, project planning and project scheduling

Quality management
- the dimensions of quality
- inspecting and sampling for quality
- Total Quality Control (TQC) and Total Quality Management (TQM)

Controlling operations
- controlling processes
- inventory

Human resources management
- job evaluation
- wages
- ergonomic factors
- people and machines

Purchasing
Quality of material
- suitability for use
- price
- availability

Quantity of material
- continuity of supply
- minimum investment in stocks
- conforming to safety and economic requirements
- maintenance of records of demand and prices

Time
- buying at right time to gain price advantages
- delivery at agreed dates

Prices
- purchasing at lowest price consistent with quality and service
- balancing low purchase prices against other factors, e.g. higher costs in use

Source
- selecting suppliers
- evaluating suppliers
- avoiding dependence on one supplier

RESEARCH AND DEVELOPMENT

Source: in-house or bought-in
Cost: expenditure
Methods
- design new ideas
- testing new products or processes

Effect: link of R&D effort to profitability and performance
Managing R&D
- achieving innovation
- implementing new ideas

SALES

Sales personnel
- number of staff
- selecting
- training
- rewarding

Sales techniques
- communication and contact with existing and potential buyers
- support from marketing and other departments
- making deals
- order processing
- Sales results
- sales
- profitability
- cost of sales

> **DISCUSSION**
> Choose one of the areas above and discuss what implications the range of functions might have for the language and communication needs of students. For example:
>
> Research & Development: in-house or bought-in training source?
> If a company has its own in-house R&D function, a team of people will have to be managed and this will involve a wide range of language and communication (handling meetings, making presentations and maybe writing reports).
> If a company out-sources its R&D, it will have to communicate with a range of suppliers – for example, university departments, private labs etc. This will involve meetings, presentations and written communication but externally rather than internally.

BUSINESS SECTORS

In the Organisations in Business section, we saw that one way into the content of Business English is through the organisation of the company and an individual's function within the hierarchy. The question: What do you do? would be likely to yield some information about position and function. However, the response to the same question could include information about the individual's company, for example:

- I work for a pharmaceutical company.
- I'm a partner in a law firm.
- I'm responsible for a team of portfolio managers in a bank.

Here the key information is the business sector in which the individual works.

The structure of a company, as shown by the organigram, will show a series of linked boxes with power flowing from senior management through the managerial ranks. However, the hierarchy is a complete picture. There are no loose ends – at least not in the flowchart. In contrast, the list of business sectors is huge and there is very little or no overlap between areas. So, while the list of company departments is closed-ended, the list of business sectors is virtually open-ended (as a quick look at the Yellow Pages will show). However, the list below is another starting point for exploring content areas in Business English. For the in-company trainer working in a single business environment, it is easier to develop some knowledge about the company's activities. For the teacher required to work with participants from many different areas, understanding the range of professional sectors represents a real challenge, as is shown from the list of business sectors on the next page.

MANUFACTURING		SERVICE	
Aerospace	Furniture	Accounting	Law
Agriculture	Gas	Advertising	Medicine
& food production	Mining	Architecture	Military
Automotive	Petroleum	Banking & finan-	Music
Chemical	Pharmaceutical	cial services	Politics &
Clothing &	Plastics	Communication	government
footwear	Power	services	Printing
Construction	generation	(including	Real estate
Cosmetics &	Pulp & paper	broadcasting)	Security &
personal care	Rail	Consultancy	protection
Dyes & pigments	Road	Environment	Tax
Electrical	Rubber	Health & healthcare	Tourism
Electronics	Telecoms	Hotels & restaurants	Training
Energy	Textiles	Insurance	(including
Engineering	Water	International relations	education)
Food & drink		& organisations	Transportation
		International trade	(including
			shipping)
		Journalism	Utilities

> **DISCUSSION**
> Choose two or three of the above business sectors:
> 1 What products or services do they provide?
> 2 Who are the customers?
> 3 Which companies have a major presence in your area?

3 The Language of Business English

In Chapter 1, we explored the scope of Business English and I stated that the legitimate scope of our pedagogic activities as Business English trainers is to design and deliver courses which aim to increase language knowledge and communication skills.

In this chapter, we will look in more detail at two areas of language knowledge: grammar, and vocabulary. The third area, pronunciation, will not be covered in this book as there are no specific rules relating to the pronunciation of Business English.

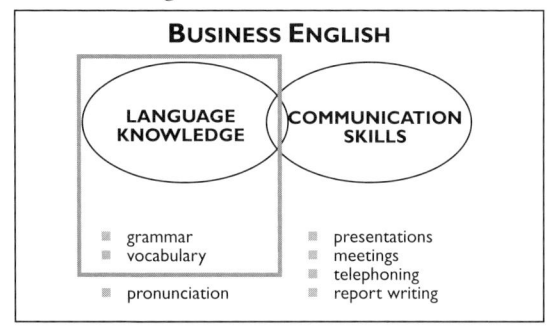

BUSINESS ENGLISH

LANGUAGE KNOWLEDGE
- grammar
- vocabulary
- pronunciation

COMMUNICATION SKILLS
- presentations
- meetings
- telephoning
- report writing

Grammar

Is there a grammar of Business English? To answer this question, we first of all need to decide what grammar is. Here are two definitions:
1 the rules and conventions of language shared by a group of native speakers
2 the structure of the categories of language.

Under the first point, we can debate whether a particular language form is right or wrong in standard language, i.e. whether it is grammatically correct. Under the second point, learners study the A – Z of grammatical structures.

Grammatical accuracy is, in most cases, black or white. The rules of grammar point unambiguously to the mistakes in the following sentences:
- This presentation will covers…
- I have divided my talk into four mains point
- Let's look on the first point

There are, of course, some grey areas, even in standard language. As a result, educated native speakers of standard British English might have differing views about the correctness of:
- There's three companies in the group
- Is it you or me who should sign this report?
- Can you speak a little slower, please.

In one sense, as least, language is a living entity. And, as it develops, yesterday's grey areas change their hue, while new grey areas appear, adding to the ammunition of the language purists campaigning against language change.

Another dimension to grammatical variation can be found in some specific varieties, such as British English, American English, Australian English, Indian English, West African English. A typical contrast can be seen in the following pair of sentences:
- I've already finished the report. (BrE)
- I already finished the report. (AmE)

But in the arena of grammar, both the grey areas and the geographical differences pale into numerical insignificance when compared to the indisputable cases of convergence between speakers of standard language. The rules of grammar are set in fairly solid stone. As a result, language teachers may feel reasonably confident about correcting 'mistakes' in the language produced by their students.

With regard to the question about the existence of a grammar of Business English, I do not think that there are any language categories specific to Business English. Business English can utilise all the language forms which exist in General English: the nouns, verbs, adjectives, adverbs, prepositions and determiners; none are excluded. Similarly there are no new categories which have been created for Business English. What one may find, however, is that certain grammatical forms are more prevalent or less prevalent in Business English discourse patterns or genres.

In analysing the grammatical forms of a language, much attention has traditionally been paid to phrases, clauses and sentences. Discourse, however, looks at patterns of language beyond the level of the sentence to see how different parts are 'chunked together' in order to create a coherent and cohesive whole. Discourse studies focus on areas such as:
- connections and transitions between ideas
- connections and transitions between sentences
- connections between clauses
- turn-taking in conversation
- establishing a new topic of conversation.

Discourse patterns vary between different uses and users. The discourse of spoken colloquial language will reveal very different features from the discourse of a written technical manual. Compare the following examples:
1. You can use whatever type of paper you like. The printer will work anyway.
2. The printer will work with all paper types.

The meaning in both sentences is that the printer will work irrespective of the paper used. However, the sentence structure varies. Example 1 is more typical of spoken language; example 2 is more neutral and could be used in both a spoken and a written form

In addition, each of us has our own individual features or idiosyncrasies in speech and writing. These may well be identified as a penchant for using (or overusing) a particular grammatical form. However, except in very restricted discourse (e.g. instructions) or specialist discourse (e.g. contracts), the language categories will include the familiar panoply of nouns, verbs, articles, prepositions, etc. A detailed frequency analysis may reveal that certain grammatical categories are more widely used in one type of discourse than in another, but a thorough analysis is unlikely to find the absence of a whole category. In this respect, the grammar of Business English needs to cover all the core grammatical areas of general English.

While discourse looks at ways of establishing coherence and cohesion in longer chunks of spoken or written text according to form and function, genre analysis focuses on communicative acts according to their communicative purpose. A typical example is a newspaper advertisement. Put in front of a group of people who share the same cultural conditioning, it will be recognised for its communicative purpose. In other words, the viewers would be able to recognise the link between the form of the advertisement and its objective(s). By extension, genre analysis looks not at the linguistic form but at the uniquely shared features of specific communicative purposes or communication acts. In Business English, this could include activities such as product presentations, briefing meetings, internal informational memos or cold-contact promotional letters, each of which could be recognised and classified according to its communicative purpose. But is there a grammar of Business English genres? Is there a specific subset of language patterns which are unique to product presentations or product advertisements? Again, I feel that there may be language forms which predominate in a written or spoken text, and that these patterns may well be characteristic of that particular text. However, Business English, as a wide-ranging area encompassing all communication activities used in business interactions has no limits as far as grammar is concerned. So, while specific genres may have distinctive grammatical patterns, Business English is characterised by the full range of forms.

VOCABULARY

Vocabulary represents the main building blocks of functional meaning in language. The list of words in English is huge. The most nearly complete dictionary of the language, the *Oxford English Dictionary* (13 volumes, 1933) contains 500,000 words in English. It has been estimated, however, that the present English vocabulary consists of more than one million words, including slang and dialect expressions and scientific and technical terms, many of which only came into use after the middle of the twentieth century. The English language is said to contain more than half a million words. Yet the average native speaker is able to get by with around 5,000. The words are bound together by grammar, but without words, normal interaction fails.

The York Associates Teaching Business English Handbook

Business English, inasmuch as it covers areas and topics not commonly used by general speakers, has its own specialist vocabulary. And, as in general English, vocabulary is central to communication where clearly defined topics are under consideration. So, how can we forecast the vocabulary that will be needed for different topics to be covered in business interaction? One starting point is to identify the types of, or contexts for communication. These may be summarised as follows:

1. specialist → specialist
2a. specialist → non-specialist
2b. non-specialist → specialist
3. generalist → generalist

1 Specialist to specialist. This presupposes the need for a range of vocabulary dealing with shared professional issues. The precise lexical items required will depend on the topic under consideration. However, it is possible to predict the range of specialist vocabulary needed to treat topics within key management areas.

2 Specialist to non-specialist / non-specialist to specialist. Today's broadly based professionals will need to be equipped to handle a wide range of management issues both within and outside their specialist areas. The increasing importance of team working and multi-disciplinary workgroups has led to a need for the multi-faceted manager. Multi-skilling includes language knowledge. To be effective in such a work environment, managers need the vocabulary knowledge not only of their own areas, but also of other areas of the company's operations.

3 Generalist to generalist. This refers to the wider contexts in which professionals communicate outside the strict confines of corporate offices and boardrooms. A popular maxim is that successful business relationships are built on successful personal relationships. So the social side of communication must not be ignored – the ability to converse about social, economic, political, environmental and personal issues. And this competence required its own set of vocabulary.

In addition to the context-driven and topic-driven vocabulary, there is clearly a need for 'general purpose vocabulary', derived from a common core of basic terms. This latter approximates to the language taught on general English programmes, although there will be some overlap between terms from the common core and those for generalist to generalist communication.

While vocabulary lists can be daunting for the learner, they are a useful starting point for exploring the range of terms drawn from key areas within business. Of course, the role of the trainer is to serve the terms in digestible chunks. The word lists in the Checklist on specialist vocabulary in Part 3 of this book are offered as a way in to the specialist language of Business English.

4 Communication Skills in Business

Accuracy, Fluency and Effectiveness

In Chapter 1, we explored the scope of Business English and I stated that the legitimate scope of our pedagogic activities as Business English trainers is to design and deliver courses which aim to increase language knowledge and/or communication skills. In the same chapter we looked at learners' objectives, which I summarised as aiming to develop one or more of the following:

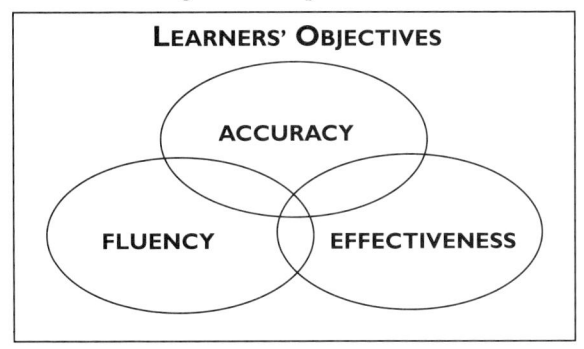

LEARNERS' OBJECTIVES

- ACCURACY
- FLUENCY
- EFFECTIVENESS

Accuracy

Linguistic accuracy is, in most cases, black or white. The rules of grammar state what is right and teachers, in contrast, (are often asked to) point out what is wrong. In the domain of vocabulary, a word is either right or wrong in a particular context. It is only at the level of pronunciation that foreign learners' efforts to approximate to the sound system of English are allowed greater latitude, as the goal of achieving native-speaker pronunciation is regarded as unrealistic.

ACCURACY OF LANGUAGE KNOWLEDGE

- words
- grammar
- pronunciation

However, when we look at fluency and effectiveness, the same categories of black and white do not apply. Rather we are looking at a cline with zero competence at one end and native-speaker competence at the other. In the middle are many levels of fluency. The same is true for effectiveness, which, in professional communication, is different from fluency. So accuracy is yes/no, while fluency and effectiveness are more/less. What makes the assessment of fluency and effectiveness so problematic is the absence of scientifically measurable criteria against which to grade performance.

FLUENCY

> **FLUENCY OF COMMUNICATION**
>
> - speed of speaking
> - effort of speaking

The word 'fluency' is derived from the Latin verb *fluere*, meaning to flow. The Concise Oxford Dictionary defines the adjective 'fluent' as 'expressing oneself quickly and easily'. 'Speed of speaking' is, indeed, objectively measurable, but there is no agreed 'speed limit' within which speech should flow. Listeners will largely agree on which speakers are outside acceptable bounds; where a speaker is groping for words so that there are uncomfortable gaps in delivery; or where a speaker rattles on in English without concern for the comprehensibility of the message. So rather than a single standard of fluency, there is a range of delivery speeds within the 'fluent' band. We need also to consider individual differences. All native speakers have their own natural 'speed of speaking' – some faster, some slower; and this speed will itself vary, depending on the situation and topic. So, what might be a natural delivery speed for speaker A in context Y might well be quite different from speaker B in context Z.

It is the perception of the listener(s) which lies at the heart of fluency. Does the speaker achieve a natural flow in the language? If they feel that a speaker is speaking too slowly, their impression will be of lack of fluency. Yet among non-native speakers, there could, indeed, be a real advantage to 'slow' speech since it could aid the comprehension of listeners. For example, if a non-native speaker speaks at a relatively slow speed – slower than a comparable native speaker talking about the same subject – the listeners may not notice the lack of fluency or may consider the speaker to be fluent since the slowness of delivery helps them to decode the message. So speed is a variable rather than an absolute factor of fluency.

The second criterion in the dictionary definition is 'ease of speaking'. Here we are talking about the effort of speakers in formulating their message. But how are we to measure effort? The only way is to ask the speaker about the level of difficulty experienced. So how is this to be validated and how can it be compared between speakers? It is clear that fluency, one of the objectives often expressed by learners of both general and Business English, has no scientifically measurably basis and depends on purely impressionistic features of speech.

EFFECTIVENESS

> **EFFECTIVENESS OF PROFESSIONAL COMMUNICATION**
>
> - impact of delivery
> - variety of media
> - conciseness of communication

General English courses tend to focus on developing accuracy and fluency. Business English programmes, influenced as they are by communication skills training, also need to concern themselves with the criterion of effectiveness.

While the key word for fluency is flow, the core of effectiveness is impact. Effectiveness is a stylistic feature of communication. It is at once part of the message and part of the medium. One speaker may kill an altogether interesting message by ineffective delivery; yet an effective communicator can bring even the most mundane message to life. As with fluency there are no absolute rules of effectiveness. What works for speaker A may seem totally inappropriate for speaker B. In the middle there are a number of behavioural parameters to be experimented with in order to achieve a style which is both comfortable and effective. In the training room, the trainee can separate the techniques from the message and work on strategies that have the required audience impact.

Like fluency, the elements of effective communication are not susceptible to scientific measurement. They include behavioural features, such as:
- use of hand and arm gestures
- use of eye contact
- vocal variety
- use of visual aids

The York Associates Teaching Business English Handbook

- movement within the audience area
- handling questions
- handling difficult audiences.

Effective communicators will develop their own strategies and techniques – personal styles which transcend the use of a foreign language, but which can enhance the message of many less fluent and less accurate language users.

So these three objectives – accuracy, fluency and effectiveness – require different knowledge and skills. I have taught many learners who have been at very different 'levels' on each of these scales. There have been those who have built up an impressive knowledge of language forms, particularly in terms of grammar and vocabulary. And given time and tolerance on the part of the listener, they can produce well-formed (accurate) language. However, they have neither fluency (smooth flow), nor effectiveness (impact). Another category includes those who are fluent, yet inaccurate. They can express their ideas and convey information by filling all the uncomfortable gaps with noise, yet their communication lacks focus and impact and is marred by lapses in basic linguistic accuracy. The third group is characterised by those who can communicate effectively for short periods. They have (mastered) the techniques of effective communication, especially in presentations, but have, in fact, only limited linguistic tools at their disposal. Once outside their specialist area, their competence rapidly declines as the gaps in language knowledge needed to express their ideas become more apparent.

In this section, we will look in more detail at the core professional communication skills listed below.

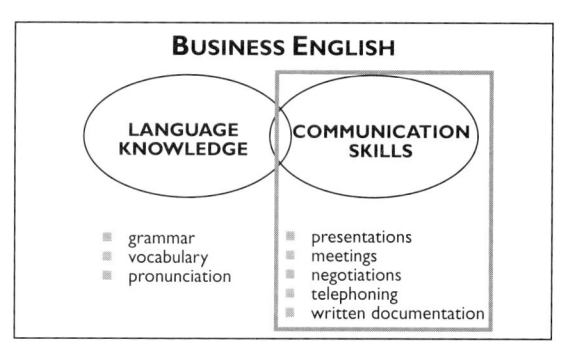

BUSINESS ENGLISH

LANGUAGE KNOWLEDGE
- grammar
- vocabulary
- pronunciation

COMMUNICATION SKILLS
- presentations
- meetings
- negotiations
- telephoning
- written documentation

All learners will agree that these skills are central to the communication of today's business professional. And many trainees will see their reason for attending a training course in terms of improving these skills. What is more difficult to pin down is the precise meaning of 'improve'. Some learners see improvement in terms of better language control and fewer mistakes, i.e. accuracy; others see it in terms of greater spontaneity and more flow, i.e.

fluency; and a third group see it in terms of impact on listeners, i.e. effectiveness. Many will ideally want to improve in all areas. But, as trainers, we need to provide a realistic service and guide learners towards a practical compromise in which they can improve (and register their improvement) within the learning parameters set by the course – duration, intensity, group size, etc.

PRESENTATIONS

A presentation is a talk given by one individual to one or more listeners. The exact format is not clearly defined and can include anything from a rigidly-formatted ten minute conference talk about new techniques in cardiovascular surgery, to a loosely-structured three-day training session on a new piece of telecoms equipment. However, in all cases it should be prepared for a specific target audience. This is the starting point for preparation, whether the presentation is to be given in the learner's first language or in English.

Presentation training in Business English may be offered either as a short course in its own right or as part of a longer Business English programme. In both cases, the trainer should aim to give every participant at least one opportunity to give a full presentation. In my experience, 15 minutes is a good length of time for a speaker to practise using the techniques for effective presentation.

While preparation is the starting point for a good presentation, trainees on in-service courses usually prefer to focus on the practical skills required to deliver a message to an audience. And though learners may perceive these skills in terms of improving their accuracy or their fluency or their effectiveness, they generally see the classroom as an arena for practising and getting feedback on their performance. Thus the feedback given may focus on one or more of these areas.

The key to improving overall performance is firstly to agree what constitutes an effective presentation. The following model seems to resonate with most learners and provides a useful template for performance feedback and evaluation.

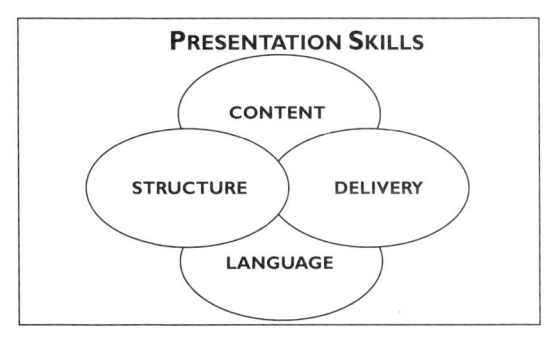

PRESENTATION SKILLS

- CONTENT
- STRUCTURE
- DELIVERY
- LANGUAGE

Content refers to the information that the speaker has chosen to convey. Has the speaker made a good choice in terms of:
- level (does the presentation correspond with the needs and interests of the majority of the audience?)
- quantity (does the speaker attempt to convey an appropriate amount of information in the available time?)
- accuracy (is the information correct?)

Structure refers to the organisation of the information chosen into an overall package – the presentation. Is it effective in terms of:
- organisation of presentation (does the presentation have a clear beginning, middle and end?)
- transparency of organisation (is the structure of the presentation clearly signalled to the audience so that they can see the beginning, middle and end?)

Delivery refers to the techniques used by the speaker to have an impact on the audience. Is there effective use of:
- voice (is there enough variety of volume and tempo to maintain audience interest?)
- body language (does the speaker appear open, confident, interested, etc.?)
- eye contact (does the speaker establish rapport with the audience?)
- visual aids (is there sufficient support to reinforce the speaker's message? does the speaker make good use of the support chosen?)

Language refers to the traditional categories of language forms, which are the main tools to communicate the message. Are these used correctly, particularly in terms of the:
- grammar
- vocabulary
- pronunciation?

In order to derive the greatest benefit from classroom time on short courses, it is important that trainees are told to prepare their presentations in advance and to bring with them any visual aids to support their presentation. This means that once the elements of effective presentation have been agreed, classroom activities move through a series of mini-practice sessions in which the learners aim to improve their performance in an observable way in one or more of the above areas.

Below are the objectives of a typical presentation skills programme, run as a two-day course for a group of in-service professionals, and agreed by trainees at the beginning of a course.

COURSE OBJECTIVES
- To develop presentation skills in terms of effective organisation

Background Issues in Business and Business English

- To improve presentation techniques in order to have greater impact on the audience
- To learn appropriate expressions for presentations
- To practise presentations and get feedback on strengths and weaknesses
- To review design and exploitation of visual aids.

It is important to point out that the area of content rarely features in the course objectives identified by trainees at the beginning of a course. This does not mean that it is not commented on during feedback sessions. In fact, where the trainees come from the same professional area, a lot of feedback deals with the complexity, quantity and accuracy of information. However, content training is not within the scope of the Business English trainer's remit, though, of course, it is a vital concern for the trainees.

Central to the programme development is the following model, which is used as a flexible guide for the practice sessions during the course.

PRESENTATION BUILDING BLOCKS

Based on these course objectives and the building blocks of the presentation, the programme would move through the following stages:

1 Elements of effective presentation. Video model followed by round table discussion.
2 Structure of presentation. Discussion of presentation building blocks (see above)
3 Practice 1. Each participant gives a two-minute presentation. This covers:
   - greeting the audience
   - giving an introduction of themselves and their talk
   - outlining the main points of the talk.

   Each practice is followed by feedback around the table on content, structure, delivery and language – both strengths and weaknesses. Where necessary, a participant may be asked to repeat this part.
4 Transparency of presentation structure and link phrases. Discussion of importance of signalling structure to audience and focus on key phrases.
5 Practice 2. Each participant gives a ten-minute presentation of the main part of their prepared talk. Each practice is followed by feedback around the table

```
Greeting
Introduce yourself
        ↓
Introduce your talk
        ↓
Outline talk
        ↓
Present main part
divided into:
Point 1
Point 2
Point 3
        ↓
Summarise
main points
        ↓
Conclude talk
        ↓
Invite questions
```

on content, structure, delivery and language. This practice session is typically videoed so that participants can view (part of) their performance. (As working through six or more presentations in succession can get boring, this practice can be divided into two or more parts.)

6   Visual aids. Discussion of good and bad overhead transparencies; discussion of good and bad exploitation of overhead transparencies.
7   Practice 3. Each participant presents a transparency (2 – 3 minutes), practising
    - appropriate language
    - appropriate techniques.
    Each practice is followed by feedback around the table on delivery and language.
8   Body language. Discussion of appropriate techniques.
9   Summarising and concluding. Discussion of importance of a strong and memorable ending.
10 Practice 4. Each participant summarises and concludes their presentation. Feedback as before.
11 Practice 5. Each participant gives a complete presentation. Feedback as before.
12 Question handling. Discussion of place for questions (during or after presentation), techniques and language for handling both easy and difficult questions.
13 Practice 6. Each participant gives part of their prepared talk, while the audience interrupts with questions. Feedback as before.
14 Practice 7. If time permits, further practice of part of the presentation, the complete presentation or another complete or part presentation. Feedback as before.

For a list of linking phrases for presentations, see the Checklist at the back of the book.

Training can help presenters improve the effectiveness of their presentation skills. By focusing on the four areas of content, structure, delivery and language, presenters can increase their confidence in their ability to achieve the desired result from their message. Training undoubtedly improves communication skills. And in particular, presentation structure and delivery can be improved quite markedly through classroom practice and constructive feedback. In general, all presenters can make noticeable progress in a short time in targeted areas and complete a course with clearly improved skills.

While training helps to improve performance, there are those communicators who defy the conventional common-sense approach to communication skills. They give memorable performances simply by breaking the rules which most less confident people find helpful. Giving a commendable performance is, in my experience, within the grasp of every presenter, but giving a memorable presentation requires basic communication techniques plus a good measure of performing talents. While the former can be developed quite rapidly by means of training, the latter is something which an individual basically either has or has not got.

For those trainers working with trainees whose aim is to achieve a commendable performance, here is a short list of tips:

The Five Principles of Effective Presentation

1 The principle of clear structure. Your communication should have a clear beginning, middle and end.

2 The principle of multimedia. Your audience will remember better and longer if there are multiple stimuli.

3 The principle of two-way communication. Your communication will be more effective if you audience have an opportunity to participate actively.

4 The principle of cultural sensitivity. Remember and pay attention to the sensitivities of your audience.

5 The principle of memory. People tend to remember the information they heard last (and forget what was said at the beginning of the talk).

DISCUSSION
1 Think of the memorable presentations that you have heard. What was it that made the performance memorable?
2 Do you agree that presentation techniques can be taught?
3 Patterns of communication vary between cultures. Do you think presenters should try to adopt the cultural communication patterns of the audience to which they are speaking?

MEETINGS

Business people spend a lot of time in meetings. In fact many would argue 'too much time'. Although part of their frustration stems from the view that meetings are often seen as preventing them from 'real work', there is also a genuine feeling that many meetings are badly run. Streamlining procedures and improving outputs are, therefore, highly desirable goals.

As with presentations, the exact format of a meeting is not clearly defined and there are many types of gatherings which may be classed as meetings:

Briefing meetings. Here the purpose is to inform others of a new development, new procedures or a new solution. Obtaining the views of the participants is not central to the purpose of the meeting.

Brainstorming meetings. Here the aim is to collect ideas from all participants around the table. Often the ideas are given randomly, without evaluation of their appropriacy.

Decision-making and problem-solving meetings. Here the aim is to reach a decision or solve a problem. The meeting provides the participants with an opportunity to present their views, persuade or dissuade and finally make a decision.

Committee meetings. The meeting is attended by two or more interest groups. A chair is elected and decisions are reached by a majority vote.

Company meetings. The annual general meeting (AGM) is a legal requirement for all companies and involves fixed procedures, including the chair's (usually the chairman's) report, the company's accounts and resolutions. In addition to the general meeting, a company may call a 'special meeting' to deal with one or more specific topics.

Although business meetings don't have a fixed format, they should have the following characteristics:

> The **gathering together**
> of a **group of people**
> for a **controlled discussion**
> with a **specific purpose**

It is the last two points in the definition which differentiate a business meeting from a social meeting and which, if followed, help to ensure the effectiveness of the procedures and the success of the outcome.

Meeting training in Business English may be offered either as a short course in its own right or as part of a longer Business English programme. In both cases, the trainer should aim to provide opportunities for both controlled and free practice, as well as sharing feedback on the successes and failures of the techniques used.

While preparation is not a guarantee of a successful outcome, most meeting participants would agree that if the pre-meeting procedures have been carried out, then there is, at least, a better chance of satisfactory outcome. The list of pre-meeting tasks includes:
- deciding who is to attend
- deciding on time and place
- preparing the meeting room (tables, chairs, flipchart, audio-visual equipment)

- inviting participants
- preparing the agenda
- circulating documentation.

These preparatory activities are rarely the concern of Business English trainees. Their interest, as far as training is concerned, is to focus on the practical skills required to control meetings (as chairperson) and to contribute to meetings (as participants). And the classroom is seen as an arena for practising and getting feedback on their performance in terms of accuracy, fluency and effectiveness (or a combination of these parameters). These criteria should, therefore, be the basis for meeting training, meeting practice and meeting feedback.

The key to improving performance is firstly to agree on what constitutes an effective meeting. The following model, though not exhaustive, captures many points which are relevant to different types of meeting. And, as with the corresponding model for effective presentations, it provides a useful template for performance feedback and evaluation.

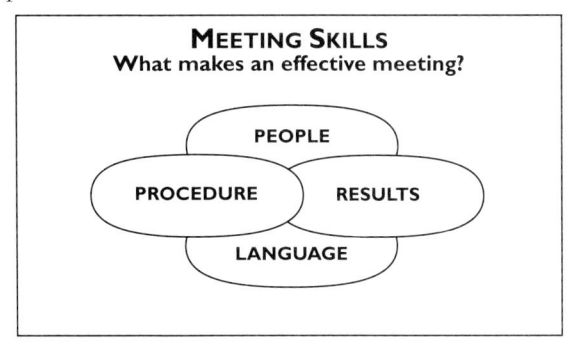

MEETING SKILLS
What makes an effective meeting?

PEOPLE / PROCEDURE / RESULTS / LANGUAGE

People refers to everyone involved in the meeting and their roles:
- the chairperson / the participants / the secretary
- the boss / the subordinate
- the expert / the non-expert.

Are the right people present in order to achieve the purpose of the meeting? Do they know what roles they are expected to fulfil.

Procedures refers to the steps and stages of the meeting and their management.
1 The chairperson is responsible for overall control, in particular:
- opening the meeting
- stating the purpose/objectives of the meeting
- introducing items on the agenda
- agreeing the ground rules for the meeting (contributions, timing, decision-making, etc.)
- asking for contributions

- involving all the participants
- keeping the meeting on target (time, relevance, decisions)
- clarifying, when necessary
- summarising, when necessary
- closing the meeting.

2 The participants are responsible for:
- making relevant contributions
- observing the agreed procedures for the conduct of the meeting.

3 The secretary is responsible for:
- keeping a record of participants present, points discussed, conclusions reached and actions to be taken
- distributing the minutes within a reasonable time.

Are all these stages managed effectively?

Results refers to the outcomes of the meeting. A lot of meetings fail because the participants are unsure of the purpose and therefore dissatisfied with the results. Therefore effective meetings depend entirely on:
- communicating the purpose
- satisfying expectations
- clarifying the outcome in terms of action.

Language refers to the traditional categories of language forms:
- grammar
- vocabulary
- pronunciation.

Are these used correctly?

In order to derive the greatest benefit from classroom time on short courses, it is important that classroom activities focus on meeting practice and feedback. This means that once the elements of effective meetings have been agreed, classroom activities move through a series of mini-practice sessions in which the learners aim to improve their performance in an observable way in one or more of the above areas.

Below are the objectives of a typical meeting skills programme, run as a three-day course for a group of in-service professionals.

COURSE OBJECTIVES
- To develop meeting skills in terms of effective procedures
- To improve techniques for controlling and participating in meetings
- To practise presenting information at meetings
- To learn appropriate expressions for controlling and participating in meetings
- To practise meetings and get feedback on strengths and weaknesses

So, referring to the effective meetings template, the main concerns of typical

Business English learners can be summarised as:
- the procedural elements
- the linguistic elements
- practice
- feedback.

These learning objectives can be translated into a training programme in meeting skills based around the following procedural steps, which can be used as a flexible guide for the practice sessions during the course.

1 Procedures for the chairperson
- Open the meeting
- State purpose/objectives of meeting
- Welcome new participants, if necessary
- Give apologies for absence
- Read secretary's report of last meeting
- Deal with Matters Arising from report
- Introduce agenda for current meeting and review/amend/prioritise, as necessary
- Introduce item 1 and invite oral report
- Invite discussion, if appropriate
- Summarise points discussed
- Lead into decision-making process, if appropriate
- Conclude point and thank presenter
- Introduce next item and invite report, until all points have been covered or time has run out
- Summarise points covered and decisions made. Relate to objectives
- Invite Any Other Business (AOB)
- Agree time, date and place for next meeting
- Thank participants for attending
- Close meeting
- Go through agenda

2 Procedures for the participants
- Present information in the form of an oral report or mini-presentation
- Participate in discussion, involving:
   ...giving and seeking opinions
   ...interrupting
   ...commenting
   ...agreeing and disagreeing
   ...advising and suggesting
   ...requesting information and action
   ...checking and confirming information.

3 Procedures for the secretary. To record:
- the names of the participants
- the topics discussed

- brief details of arguments for and against
- decisions made
- voting details
- follow-up actions to be carried out (who, what and when)
- the date, time and place of the next meeting.

The above procedures are fairly exhaustive. Many meetings (e.g. brainstorming) will not be bound by procedures. However, the complete communicator will need a command of these procedures so that they can be drawn on as and when necessary. Some are relatively mechanical (welcoming participants) whilst others (summarising) involve complex skills. Improving a student's ability to summarise will mean looking at the way information and ideas can best be structured; in order to handle the decision-making process in a meeting, students need to show both understanding and decisiveness at critical moments. Effective management of or participation in a meeting can be achieved if trainees are firstly made aware of the process of meetings and then given a set of tools to guide them through this process. The tools which enable these procedures to be effectively carried out are mainly linguistic, involving oral and written communication. The list of phrases in the checklist at the back of the book shows the language corresponding to the steps to be carried out.

Before looking at the phrases themselves, it is useful to put them into some of functional context, according to the purpose(s) they fulfil. While link phrases for presentations (see checklist), signal to the audience, as he/she moves through his/her presentation, recent and planned progress, the forms required by the chairperson are 'control language' so that the meeting participants know what stage the meeting has reached and what steps they are expected to take next. As with the earlier list of link phrases, the 'control phrases' in the checklist are intended to start trainees thinking of the kind of language suitable for meeting procedures. The list is not complete: trainees should explore the range of phrases and, in the light of the type and climate of the meeting, choose those that best suit them, and the context.

Training can help improve the effectiveness of skills by focusing on the procedural and linguistic elements involved in running and participating in meetings. Beyond the control language is, of course, the heart of the meeting itself – the topics to be discussed. For meeting skills to be practised, agendas of points for discussion need to be drawn up. There are basically two approaches – student-generated or teacher-generated. Where students share the same professional background, it usually requires little effort to get them to draw up a list of key points for discussion, information- or opinion-exchange or even decision-making. These points can then be fashioned into an agenda around which to practise meeting skills.

Where the trainees come from different areas and backgrounds, the trainer will often need to provide an agenda. Points must necessarily reflect issues of universal interest. The following sample list includes items of human, ethical and practical concern, all of which can engage trainees and provide a platform for serious discussion.

AGENDA FOR A SIMULATED MEETING

Inter-Departmental Liaison Committee Meeting
Agenda

Item One - Environmentally Friendly Office
Your company has decided to take part in a national survey to determine how environmentally friendly the nation's top companies are. Before the environmental audit, you want to improve the current situation. What can be done? You already have some ideas, you would like some more.
Proposed measures:
- Incentives to encourage staff to use public transport
- Reduction of building temperature by 5°C
- Recycling bins for waste materials

Item Two - Japanese Visitors
A group of twenty visitors from the Japanese Ministry of Industry is visiting your company. They are in your area to look at the feasibility of setting up a new car plant. Inward investment is desparately needed in your region. Plan the one day visit for the Japanese group. Try to include a mix of business and culture.

Item Three - A Mission Statement
As part of an ongoing public relations drive, you have decided to create a new mission statement which will represent your company's values through to the year 2000. Decide what this mission statement should be, the values that it represents and how best to communicate it to your employees and your customers.

Item Four - Business Gifts
It is clear that staff who have direct contact with the customer have been accepting rather large business gifts, for example cases of high quality single malt Scotch whisky. It is clear that the company needs to establish clearer guidelines on what is and what is not acceptable.

Item Five - Training Budget
Due to rather poor results last year, the training budget has had to be reduced. You need to establish the relative priorities of technical, management and language training. Consider the relative merits and allocate the budget on a percentage basis.

Item Six - Internet
Your company made the Internet and World Wide Web available to its employees last month. However, the costs are proving to be enormous. Employees are spending both worktime and freetime on the Internet, running up large bills and reducing their efficiency at work. You need to consider the pros and cons of your first decision and perhaps establish new guidelines.

The York Associates Teaching Business English Handbook

As with all communication skills, the key is practice and feedback. The trainer needs, therefore, to set up a context for communication (a practice agenda, or part of an agenda), an agreed template against which to evaluate performance (checklist of steps and procedures) and a climate in which constructive feedback can be shared around the table.

> **DISCUSSION**
> 1 Think of good meetings that you have participated in. What was it that made them good?
> 2 Do you agree that meeting techniques can be taught?
> 3 Patterns of communication vary between cultures. What problems do you think you might face when running a training course in meeting skills for participants from different national cultures?

TELEPHONING

Presentations and meetings may play very critical roles in the lives of business people, but often much of their day-to-day business is carried out over the phone.

A business phone call can be defined according to its purpose. These include:
- giving information
- requesting information
- confirming information
- making arrangements
- persuading the called party, as in telephone selling
- negotiating with the called party
- complaining to the called party.

There are two parallel structures for telephone calls, depending on whether one is the caller or the called party. These structures can be broken down into the following building blocks:

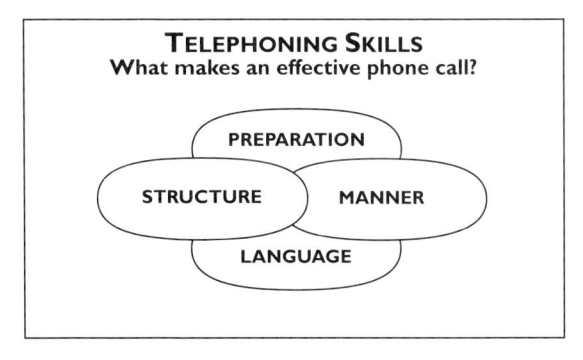

Background Issues in Business and Business English

Telephone building blocks – caller

| Greeting / Identify yourself | → to switchboard |

↓

| Request called party |

↓

| Greeting / Identify yourself | → to called |

↓

| Give reason for call |

↓

| Cover main part according to purpose
- get information
- give information
- etc. |

↓

| Pre-close call, e.g.
- summarise main points
- thank called
- respond to thanks
- etc. |

↓

| Close call |

Telephone building blocks – called

| Identify yourself | → to caller |

↓

| Cover main part according to purpose:
- give information
- make arrangements
- etc. |

↓

| Pre-close call, e.g.
- confirm main points
- thank caller
- respond to thanks
- etc. |

↓

| Close call |

These building blocks give us a starting framework for the steps or procedures involved in a phone call. For the purpose of programme development, we also need a template for evaluating performance, so that we can share feedback with our trainees. This could be based around the following model:

TELEPHONING SKILLS
What makes an effective phone call?

- PREPARATION
- STRUCTURE
- MANNER
- LANGUAGE

Preparation refers to the state of 'mental readiness' to implement the clearly-defined purpose of the call. This may be to:
- give information
- request information
- confirm information
- make arrangements
- persuade the called party
- negotiate with the called party
- complain to the called party.

Has the caller carried out the necessary preparation for an effective call? Is he/she prepared for the foreseeable range of scenarios, once he/she has dialled the number of the person being called?

Structure refers to the stages of the call. These are shown above under 'telephone building blocks'. Does the caller have an awareness of the steps to be taken to manage the call effectively, according to his/her purpose? Does the caller have the necessary skills (organisational and linguistic) to advance the call effectively through its various stages?

Manner refers to the techniques used by the parties to achieve the purpose of the call effectively. As there is no visual contact between the parties, the message relies heavily on the voice for its effective transmission. To be effective, there should be:
- clear and comprehensible speech, i.e. the speakers must avoid mumbling, jargon, complicated sentence structure, etc.
- regular and appropriate feedback, e.g. I see, I understand, uh-huh, etc.
- appropriate vocal tone for the purpose of the call, e.g. polite, helpful, persuasive, etc.
- an appropriate action during the call, i.e. don't leave the caller or the called hanging on for more than ten seconds without warning
- offers of appropriate follow-up action, where necessary.

Language refers to the traditional categories of language forms:
- grammar
- vocabulary
- pronunciation.

Are these used correctly?

As with other oral communication skills, the key to improved performance is to:
- agree on the elements of effective phone calls
- practise phone calls to integrate the elements into performance
- share feedback on strengths and weaknesses.

Although presentations and meetings are often run as training courses in their own right, telephoning typically appears as part of a wider course – either a broadly-based Business English programme or a Secretarial Skills course. Below are the possible objectives to be incorporated into the module dealing with telephone skills.

MODULE OBJECTIVES
- To develop and practise the professional communication skill of telephoning in terms of telephone manner and telephone phrases
- To practise phone calls and get feedback on strengths and weaknesses.

Practising phone calls requires both a bank of short phone exercises to be used for developing techniques and language, and longer activities requiring more detailed interaction between the parties. Published materials provide both, though where students share the same professional background, it usually requires little effort to get them to draw up a list of typical calls they need to make and receive. These can then be quite easily turned into relevant phone activities.

As with the communication skills considered earlier, the key is practice and feedback. The trainer needs, therefore, to set up contexts for communication through practice calls drawn from published material or the learners' own experiences/needs, an agreed template against which to evaluate performance (telephone building blocks and associated phrases) and a climate in which constructive feedback can be shared around the table.

> ### DISCUSSION
> 1 Think of telephone calls that you have received. What are the types of behaviour that irritate you?
> 2 What is the effect of good telephone manner?
> 3 Patterns of communication vary between cultures. What problems do you think you might face when teaching telephoning skills to participants from different national cultures?

NEGOTIATIONS

A negotiation is a special type of meeting in which the parties (usually two) need each other's agreement in order to achieve an effective result. One of the biggest problems for Business English trainers is to make sense of the competing models of negotiations offered by management gurus. These include both tactical aspects and procedural aspects, as shown in the extracts from the following negotiation programmes and models:

The York Associates Teaching Business English Handbook

---

1. The negotiating process
   Determining the basis for give and take
2. Styles
   Identifying your negotiating style
   Interpreting the styles of others
   How styles interact, conflict, or mesh
3. Pre-Negotiation Planning Steps
   Establishing your specific needs
   How to sort out your options
   Getting all of the facts
   Finding out the bottom-line need of the seller
   Identifying your "trading cards"
4. Effective Communications in Negotiations
   How to listen and what to listen for
   Communicating without emotion
   Watching for non-verbal messages and signals
   Overcoming traps, gaps, and barriers
5. Using Cost-Price Analysis as a Negotiating Asset
   How to determine the real costs
   Negotiating profits and margins
   Getting all of the financial facts
6. Dealing With Conflict Creatively
   Handling differences and disruptions
   Learning to assert yourself
   Preventing their problems from becoming your problems

From The Center for Executive Development, College of Business Administration, University of Houston, Houston, Texas, USA

---

1. The negotiation process – how negotiations develop
2. Planning negotiations – assessing power, framing objectives, defining issues, setting positions
3. The meeting – setting the climate, presenting your case, getting useful information, controlling movement, using adjournments
4. The negotiating team – advantages and possible problems, managing teams effectively
5. Influencing skills
6. Dealing with conflict – conflict in the team, conflict with the other side, indirect conflict
7. The contract – what it should contain, use in negotiation
8. Reaching agreement – ensuring implementation, building in contingencies

From Civil Service College, Larch Avenue, Ascot, Berkshire SL5 OQE, UK

---

1. Five negotiations in every negotiation:
   1. competitive 2. co-operative 3. organisational
   4. attitude/personalities 5. personal
2. The three pillars of negotiation
   1. planning 2. phases 3. behaviour
3. The Model of Communication
4. Rapport Building
   How to build trust and responsiveness, both verbally and non-verbally.
   How to pace and lead in any communication.
   Non-verbal clues
5. Leading with language
   How to move language to and from the artfully vague to the specific
6. Personality and persuasion
   How to understand other people's model of the world and how to develop the flexibility of style to influence them
7. The Seven Step Approach for planning
   1. defining the goal 2. what's happened before 3. specify objectives
   4. who's got the power 5. strategy and tactics 6. plan arguments
   7. attend to the details
8. The phases of negotiation
   1. opening stance 2. listening signal 3. adding to the proposal
   4. packaging 5. bargaining 6. closing

Performance Enhancement Ltd, UK

Negotiation training in Business English may be offered either as a short course in its own right or as part of a longer Business English programme. In both cases, the trainer should aim to provide opportunities for both controlled and free practice, as well as sharing feedback on the successes and failures of the techniques used.

All the models listed above stress the importance of pre-negotiation planning. While preparation is not a guarantee of a successful outcome, most negotiation participants would agree that lack of preparation is one of the key factors leading to failure. A list of areas for considering before the negotiation includes:

- Assessing power
- Establishing your specific needs and objectives
- How to sort out your options
- Getting all of the facts
- Defining issues
- Setting positions
- Finding out the bottom-line need of the other party.

As with the tasks in preparation for a meeting, the above activities are rarely the concern of Business English trainees. Their interest, as far as training is concerned, is to focus on the practical skills required to negotiate effectively in English. And the classroom is seen as an arena for practising and getting feedback on their performance in terms of accuracy, fluency and effectiveness (or a combination of these parameters). These criteria should, therefore, be the basis for negotiation training, negotiation practice and negotiation feedback.

The key to improving performance is firstly to agree what constitutes an effective negotiation. The following model, though not exhaustive, captures many points common to all kinds of negotiation and provides a useful template for performance feedback and evaluation.

NEGOTIATING SKILLS
What makes an effective negotiation?

- PEOPLE
- PLANNING & PROCEDURES
- RESULTS
- LANGUAGE

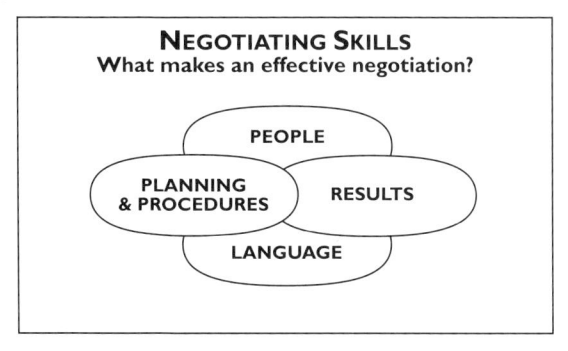

People refers to everyone involved in the negotiation and their roles, in particular:

- are all the right people present for the negotiation?
- do you have a well-balanced negotiating team?
- do both teams have decision-making power?

Planning and Procedures refers to the steps and stages of the meeting in which the negotiators meet face-to-face. These include:
- creating the right climate
- presenting the case
- collecting information
- controlling movement
- managing conflict
- summarising, when necessary
- using adjournments
- clinching the deal
- closing the meeting

Results refers to the outcomes of the negotiations. It is important that:
- all parties are committed to the agreement reached
- the terms of the agreement are clear to all parties
- the terms are capable of implementation

Language refers to the traditional categories of language forms:
- grammar
- vocabulary
- pronunciation.

In order to derive the greatest benefit from classroom time on short courses, it is important that classroom activities focus on negotiation practice and feedback. This means that once the elements of effective negotiating have been agreed, classroom activities move through a series of mini-practice sessions in which the learners aim to improve their performance in an observable way in one or more of the above areas.

Below are the objectives of a typical negotiating skills programme, run either as a three-day course for a group of in-service professionals or as part of a broadly-based Business English programme.

COURSE OBJECTIVES
- To develop negotiating skills in terms of effective procedures
- To improve negotiating techniques and tactics
- To practise presenting information in negotiations
- To learn appropriate expressions for negotiating
- To practise negotiations and get feedback on strengths and weaknesses

So, referring to the effective negotiations template, the main concerns of

typical Business English learners can be summarised as:
- the procedural elements
- the tactical elements
- the linguistic elements
- practice
- feedback.

These learning objectives can be translated into a training programme in negotiating skills based around the following model which combines both behavioural and procedural aspects:
1. Creating the right environment
2. Defining the issues
3. Establishing opening positions
4. Handling the offer and counter-offer
5. Testing the other side's case
6. Strengthening your case
7. Handling stalemate
8. Clinching the deal
9. Getting it in writing
10. The legal aspects.

The elements identified above take Business English quite far into the area of specialist communication skills and away from the traditional area of language. This is because management training providers promote success in negotiating as requiring tactical and behavioural skills, which translate into communication skills. Typically, their training products focus on a specific model with its own implicit approach. For the Business English trainer the dilemma of which model to follow can be aggravated by the possibility that learners may have followed different negotiating skills programmes as part of their earlier management training. Therefore, subscribing to someone else's model may lead to a clash of views about effective negotiations.

A safer position is to focus on the procedures and avoid the tactical manoeuvres which underpin the models presented earlier. In practice, this requires agreement on the steps involved in negotiation – a framework for practice – while leaving participants with their own tactical repertoire. In order to translate the agreed procedures into actions, trainees need a set of tools. The tools which enable these procedures to be effectively carried out are largely linguistic, involving oral and written communication. So, the suggestions in the checklist at the back of the book show the language corresponding to the steps to be carried out. As with the other lists, it is not complete, and trainees should explore the range of phrases and choose those that best suit the context in the light of the type and climate of the negotiation.

As with all communication skills, the key is practice and feedback. The trainer needs, therefore, to set up a context for communication (a practice negotiation, or part of a negotiation), an agreed template against which to evaluate performance (checklist of behavioural and procedural elements) and a climate in which constructive feedback can be shared around the table.

The contexts for negotiation can be either student- or teacher-generated. Where students share the same professional background, it usually requires little effort to get them to draw up a context for negotiation, based on their own experiences. Where the trainees come from different areas and backgrounds, the trainer will often need to provide an issue requiring negotiation. Ideally, the negotiation should be based around a problem which can be easily understood and quickly prepared. The following are examples of contexts which provide a platform for negotiating:

1 **Buyer-seller.** Negotiation over:
- price
- discount
- delivery
- payment terms.

2 **Employer-employee.** Negotiation over terms of employment, including:
- salary
- additional payments
- holiday entitlement
- additional benefits.

3 **Licensor-licensee.** Negotiation over terms of licence, including:
- financial arrangements
- geographical area
- exclusivity
- term of licence

4 **Budget allocation.** Negotiation over allocation of either company or departmental budget. The company budget negotiation could be based around the competing claims of various departments, including:
- marketing (needs more money for advertising and promotion)
- research and development (needs more money for product development)
- training (needs more money to train up company personnel)
- production (needs more money for investment in new equipment)
- administration (needs more money for new office equipment)
- etc.

DISCUSSION
1 Do you think that negotiating skills can be taught?
2 Do you agree that Business English trainers should provide training in negotiating tactics?
3 Patterns of communication vary between cultures. What problems do you think you might face when running a training course in negotiating skills for participants from different national cultures?

WRITTEN DOCUMENTATION

Written documentation can include everything from a short internal memo to a lengthy article for a journal. However, the most typical requests on Business English courses are for work on:
- correspondence (letters, faxes and e-mail)
- memos (short notes for internal consumption)
- reports
- technical documentation and specifications.

Each type of document can be compared to a communication skill in its own right with its own stylistic features according to purpose, readership and, of course, writer. However, to make sense of the area of written communication, we need some general standards to follow when teaching and also when evaluating writing performance.

At the beginning of this chapter, we introduced the factors of accuracy, fluency and effectiveness, particularly with reference to oral communication skills. The same parameters can, with modification and refocusing, be applied to written communication.

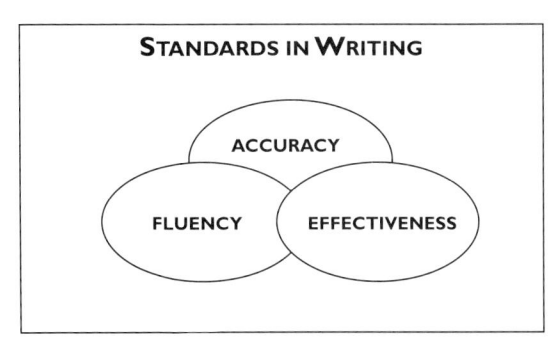

STANDARDS IN WRITING

ACCURACY

FLUENCY   EFFECTIVENESS

Accuracy refers to the correct use of language forms, in particular:
- grammar
- vocabulary
- spelling.

The York Associates Teaching Business English Handbook

Fluency refers to the mechanics required by the writer to produce a document, in particular:
- speed of writing
- effort of writing
- flow of writing.

Effectiveness refers to the impact that the finished document has on the readers in terms of:
- physical layout
- conciseness of delivery
- coherence and cohesion
- appropriacy of style
- variety of features, e.g. use of visual aids, tables and other textual and non-textual devices.

These issues translate into a range of different writing programmes, which can be run either as courses in their own right or as modules on Business English courses. Typical objectives for such courses could include:

COURSE OBJECTIVES FOR A WRITING MODULE WITHIN A SECRETARIAL SKILLS PROGRAMME

- To improve writing skills for producing commercial correspondence, especially letters and faxes
- To develop letter-writing style in terms of appropriate tone in letters and faxes
- To extend knowledge of standard phrases for commercial correspondence
- To practise writing letters and faxes and get feedback on strengths and weaknesses, especially in terms of accurate language use.

COURSE OBJECTIVES FOR A WRITING MODULE WITHIN A TECHNICAL WRITING PROGRAMME

- To improve writing skills for producing technical documentation, especially instruction manuals for equipment users
- To review parameters for effective layout of user manuals
- To develop an appropriate writing style for giving technical information and instructions, especially in terms of conciseness
- To extend knowledge of suitable phrases and structures for written technical communication
- To practise writing (parts of) technical communication and get feedback on strengths and weaknesses, especially in terms of accurate language use and effective communication style.

Course objectives for a general writing module within a Business English programme

- To improve writing skills for producing correspondence and short reports
- To develop appropriate style for correspondence and short reports
- To extend knowledge of standard phrases and structures for correspondence and report-writing
- To practise writing correspondence and short reports and get feedback on strengths and weaknesses, especially in terms of accurate language use and effective communication style

Within the scope of all writing training are the following stages:
1. agreeing the criteria for a good document and good processes for producing it
2. studying documents which represent models of good writing and discussing which features can be adapted to the trainee's own writing style
3. practising writing
4. evaluating writing according to criteria identified at stage 1.

It is outside the scope of this book to provide detailed criteria for good written documents of all types which Business English users are likely to need to write. So, the following list provides criteria which can be applied to a wide range of document types and their production. However, each item should be considered in relation to the document being written.

1. Content
- choose the correct information to be conveyed to the readers
- choose the correct quantity of information for the readers

2. Layout
   Layout is to a written document what structure is to a presentation:
- overall organisation of document should help the reader to move from introductory, general points through detail to conclusion. The structure should be clearly segmented and reinforced, where appropriate, by the use of a title and contents page, separate sections for the main body, a summary and conclusion
- appropriate use of fonts for easy readability
- consistent use of lettering in terms of font type and size, capitalisation, bold, italic, underlining; consistent use of spacing between lines, paragraphs and sections; consistent use of headings
- appropriate use of numbering, bullet marks and indentation
- appropriate use of columns and tables and other non-textual information

3. Conciseness
- use uncomplicated words and phrases
- write readable sentences by limiting their length and the quantity of information

- put information and ideas into a logical order (see also coherence below)
- use as few words as possible
- use precise words to convey the exact meaning
- make sure to edit work to make it more concise

4 Style

Style is to a written document what delivery is to a presentation
- establish the right relationship with the reader
- create credibility in the eyes of the readers
- use textual and non-textual techniques effectively to give the right impression to the readers
- use language appropriately to achieve the right tone according to the purpose of the document
- use language clearly to transmit ideas and information

5 Language
- use language forms correctly
- choose appropriate vocabulary
- remove unnecessary jargon
- ensure correct spelling and punctuation
- use abbreviation, acronyms and short forms appropriately

6 Coherence and cohesion
- ensure that overall organisation follows a logical development from beginning to end
- put linked information and ideas together
- organise the linked information and ideas into sections and paragraphs
- use a topic sentence at the beginning or end of a paragraph
- ensure that information and ideas within a section or paragraph follows a logical sequence
- use 'connectors' to link information and ideas together

7 Variety of features
- vary sentence length to avoid monotony
- vary vocabulary to maintain audience interest
- use non-textual features to reinforce or complement the message

8 Speed of writing
- limit the writing time for any document
- limit the length of any piece of writing
- use a standard format or standard wording, where possible, to reduce writing time
- use bullet points for lists rather than continuous text.

Models can provide practical examples of the above criteria. They are a good starting point for examining aspects of layout and style and learners can gain a lot from looking at well-designed and well-written documents. Of course, the objective of writing training is not for learners to replicate these models, but to adapt them to personal style and specific documents.

Therefore, the writing practice sessions should be based around:
- controlled activities to develop competence in specific formats, techniques and language
- free activities to integrate these into documents relevant to their workplace.

Published materials can provide the former; the trainees themselves the latter.

> **DISCUSSION**
> 1 How important is the written word in your culture? Are people prepared to make agreements in speech or do they prefer them in writing?
> 2 Do you think the need for writing will increase or decrease in the business community in the coming years?
> 3 Do you agree that accuracy is more important in writing than in speech?

5 Management Skills in Business

In Chapter 1, we explored the scope of Business English and I stated that the legitimate scope of our pedagogic activities as Business English trainers is to design and deliver courses which aim to increase language knowledge and/or communication skills. However, both language knowledge and communication skills are tools that enable their users to fulfil their business or management roles. So, it is important for Business English trainers to understand:
1. the professional content at the heart of the communication
2. the management context(s) in which the communication takes place.

Viewed from the latter perspective, effective communication is important for managers and their teams for two reasons:
1. It is the main process by which managers achieve their four key management activities:
   - planning
   - leading
   - organising
   - controlling.
2. It is the activity to which managers devote the majority of their time. If they are bad at it, this will have a major impact on their overall effectiveness as managers and on the general well-being of the organisation. If communication is the 'lifeblood' of the organisation, then poor communication or communication breakdowns are its 'cardio-vascular malfunctions'.

This section will provide an overview of the current preoccupations of today's managers which are considered to be at the heart of successful management:
- Leadership in order to inspire and motivate colleagues and subordinates
- Team building in order to harness the synergies of individuals brought together from different disciplines and with different specialisations
- Delegation which aims to share responsibility, empower subordinates and free up superiors.

And at the heart of these three management skills is communication.

So the objective of this chapter is to provide background knowledge for Business English teachers so that they can better understand the environments in which the tools they are teaching are used. This is different from teaching the management skills themselves, which is the role of management trainers.

LEADERSHIP

Leadership is by no means a new quality. We have had military, political and religious leaders, both good and bad, since time immemorial and history is dotted with their successes and failures. What is new is the emerging interest in business leaders. As business has come to occupy a more central role in society, we have come to recognise the importance that business leaders play in the health and wealth of the nation. And this has brought with it an interest in the managerial qualities and attributes of those who lead.

EARLY TRAIT-BASED MODELS

By definition, leadership implies an ability to get others to follow. But what lies at the heart of this exceptional skill and how does one achieve it? Early systematic approaches by psychologists focused on identifying the personal characteristics of leaders, based on the view that leaders are born, not made. These researchers studied the traits of leaders in order to identify what made them different from followers. However, these studies of leadership traits failed to uncover any features that unambiguously and consistently differentiated leaders from followers. Although leaders as a group tend to be cleverer, taller, more extroverted and more self-confident than non-leaders, these characteristics are no guarantee of effective leadership nor are they exclusive to leaders. In addition, there are leaders, such as Napoleon, who do not fit the mould. In conclusion, the weakness of the trait-based approach to leadership is that leaders do not have a single identifiable set of traits that sets them apart from non-leaders.

BEHAVIOURAL APPROACHES

Stoner, Freedman and Gilbert tell us that the failure of the trait-based approach led researchers to investigate other features, in particular behaviour. The focus in the behavioural approach was on what leaders do (or did) rather than what they are (or were). This has included analysis of activities such as:
- delegation
- communication
- motivation of the subordinates
- task completion.

The underlying idea is that as behaviour can be taught, the above leadership skills can be trained. The weakness in the behavioural approach is that effective leadership skills cannot be isolated from the business or even departmental environment in which they thrive. So what may work in one industry or with one department may not succeed when transplanted into a different context.

CONTEXT-BASED MODELS
Current management thinking favours the view that the context or situation plays an important role in the success or failure of a particular leadership style. The situational variables identified by researchers include:
- personality
- past experience
- expectations and behaviour of superiors
- expectations and behaviour of subordinates
- task requirements
- organisational culture and policies
- expectations and behaviour of peers.

The above characteristics have spawned various schools of thought on the relationship between leadership and the management situation:
1. The contingency approach attempts to identify which of these situational is most important and to predict which leadership style will be more effective in a given situation.
2. The Hersey-Blanchard situational theory of leadership suggests that leadership style should vary with the maturity of subordinates, moving through four phases as subordinates develop achievement, motivation and experience.
3. The path-goal approach focuses on managers' abilities to dispense rewards. The leadership style a manager uses will affect the types of rewards and the subordinates' perceptions of what they must do to earn those rewards.
4. The approach characterised by Fiedler suggests that leadership styles are relatively inflexible and that, therefore, leaders should be matched to an appropriate situation, not the situation changed to match the leader.
5. The transactional approach to leadership determines what subordinates need to do to achieve objectives, classifies those requirements and helps subordinates become more confident so that they can reach their objectives.
6. The transformational approach is based on the ability of leaders to motivate their team members to do more than is expected of them by raising their sense of importance and the value of the tasks. This model is based around the ability of charismatic leaders to effect major changes in a short period of time and transform major companies.
7. A recent American study by Unabridged Communications on the usage of lead, leader and leadership in selected newsprint media provides the following attributes as perceived by followers:
   - Visionary
   - Experience
   - Education
   - Accomplishment
   - A doer
   - Trusting/trustworthy (good character)
   - Risk taker
   - Innovator
   - Intelligence
   - Likeable

CURRENT DEVELOPMENTS
Research into leadership continues, moving in diverse directions, some focusing on individuals and their qualities, some on situations and their defining characteristics and some on the followers and the influences exerted on them. Experience, particularly past experience, has often been used as a primary criterion on which to judge potential leadership capability. However, research from The University of Southern California's School of Business Administration shows that traditional leadership screening based on demonstrated skills is insufficient. They suggest a new model relying on other assumptions:
- The future will require different skills from the past
- Successful executives aren't born that way but develop with experience
- Leaders need a variety of characteristics to be effective.

LEADERSHIP AND COMMUNICATION
For the purposes of the Business English teacher it is useful to note the importance attributed to leadership in today's business circles; and understand the background to the debate about innate characteristics versus learned skills. However, it is important for the Business English teacher to think about the implications of language and communication in effective leadership.

> **DISCUSSION**
> 1 Do you think that leaders are born or made?
> 2 What links are there between the qualities of a national leader and a business leader?
> 3 What is the role of language and communication in effective leadership?

TEAM BUILDING

In The *MNM Team Building Process for Printers*, Michael P. O'Connor and Becky Erickson, partners in the consulting firm, The COS Group International, have produced an excellent resource and reference material for people involved in quality and team development in any industry and any size business. Although the book addresses the management challenges of the graphic arts industry in particular, it is useful to anyone interested in step-by-step instructions for turning a staff into a self-managing team. The ideas in this section derive in large part from their work.

THE BASICS
Reduced to the simplest of definitions, team building involves combining and integrating the talents, skills and energy of individual employees to solve problems and accomplish goals and objectives that may be difficult or

impossible to achieve by management or other individual efforts alone. In essence, team building is about synergy, where the results exceed the sum of the individual input.

Basic to team building is the idea that employees are capable of taking on much greater personal accountability and responsibility. With this in mind, many day-to-day decisions that historically have fallen to the owner or manager gradually evolve into a group process in which the staff or team assumes a more participatory role. As an end result, fully developed teams will routinely come up with highly innovative solutions to complicated issues on their own, without the constant supervision and guidance of the owner or manager.

Probably the most difficult challenge to an owner/manager wanting to begin a team building initiative will be learning how to delegate decision making and transfer control to the staff. In a team-oriented business the role of the owner/manager is one of coach and resource rather than supervisor. For many owners/managers, this change in function requires a significant leap of faith and will require considerable time and effort. Yet, with faith, commitment and perseverance, experience has shown that the results are well worth the effort and anxiety.

WHY DOES TEAM BUILDING WORK?

Most successful businesses can tell you that the most effective way for a company to improve production is to focus on improving quality. Quality is determined by machines, materials, methods and people. While machines, materials and methods are important, most business owners/managers would agree that the people part of the quality equation is critical to consistently producing a quality product and providing quality service. Here's where team building has its greatest impact.

Team building improves quality for several reasons. Central to these reasons, though, is the simple fact that in the team experience the importance and value of each staff member's contribution is continually reaffirmed. In this environment of mutual respect and support, doing the right thing the first time becomes the standard, and pride in workmanship (quality) is a way of life.

As any sports fan knows, there are teams and then there are high performance teams! Here are the key characteristics and responsibilities of a high performance team member:
- Each team member has a good understanding of every other team member's individual role and function, and will at all times try to help that person be successful in their role, even if it only involves being sensitive to the problems that person may be experiencing at the time.
- Each team member understands the importance of constant communication and feedback, and is aware that to be effective, communication must move freely and openly in all directions.

- Each team member understands the value of being willing at all times to share knowledge, skills, ideas and time.
- Each team member strives to create a work environment where team members feel comfortable at all times in sharing their individual thoughts and feelings when discussing or disagreeing on an issue.

There are many other reasons and testimonials that could be given in support of the effectiveness of teams. The bottom line, however, is that by implementing a team building programme in any business, more can be done, with fewer errors, in less time than is possible in a command and control environment! That means higher sales, better profits, and ... most likely, an opportunity to take that well-deserved, worry-free vacation!

STEPS NEEDED TO DEVELOP A TEAM

Team building is not difficult work to do, although it does require certain attitudes and approaches which may be different from the way a business was traditionally managed. Before beginning to work with the staff to build a team, there are three issues to be considered.

1. **Commitment.** Commitment means being willing to devote a significant amount of time and patience to the team building initiative. Team building, unlike many management improvement schemes, is not a quick fix. It is a long term strategy of sustained and continuous improvement. Once begun, the commitment to team building will be tested numerous times while working through the process.

2. **Re-evaluation.** This means developing (or reassessing) the company's overall goals and guiding principles. Mission, vision, guiding principles and values define the purpose of and provide critical guidance in the on-going development of any business. It has been proven that people perform better when they have a clear sense of purpose, and when they know where they are going and how they are going to get there. This is true whether they are crew in a sailboat race, on the steering committee for a local festival, or part of the staff of a business. Yet for many businesses, mission, vision and guiding principles have never been formally articulated or written down. Often they exist only as partially completed thoughts tucked away in some corner of the owner's mind. It is essential, therefore, to take the time to clearly define the mission and vision of the business and then share those definitions with the staff.

3. **Sharing.** A major component of team building involves sharing the decision making process with the employees. For many businesses this may be a new experience both for the staff and for the owner/manager. Yet if approached properly, the experience shouldn't be uncomfortable. In fact, in the team building process described below, the transfer of control in decision making evolves effortlessly over a period of several months.

There are many ways in which the owner/manager can handle decision making within the company, ranging from absolute control to complete delegation. Which is best? The short answer is that most of them will yield results. When it comes to developing a high performance team, however, the participation and delegation styles will yield the best and quickest results. Many owners/managers are accustomed to making most, if not all, of the decisions. Does this mean that they cannot implement team building? No, not at all! Fortunately, a team building initiative can begin no matter what the present management style is, as long as the owner is willing to consider change and the possibility of sharing the decision making process with the staff once there is evidence that they are capable of and willing to take on this new responsibility.

How You Build a High Performance Team

When a group of people work together with a common focus, they become a team. One method (in simplified form for illustration purposes) of building the staff into a team involves the use of staff meetings where everyone participates. These meetings are very different from traditional staff meetings where the owner/manager speaks and the staff listens. Instead, during these team building staff meetings, the facilitator (who could be the owner or manager or another person with training in team building) helps the staff focus on an in-depth analysis of the company as it currently exists.

Meeting every other week over a period of several months, the staff – with the facilitator's guidance and input – explores the strengths and weaknesses of key areas of the existing business, such as facilities, equipment, products and services, vendors, customers, competition, and marketing and sales.

The objective of these meetings is to produce a "snapshot in time" of the existing business. Then, using this snapshot as a reference, the facilitator, owner/manager and staff work together to discover and explore the opportunities these strengths and weaknesses present. By the time this is done, the staff and owner are comfortable with the meetings formats and can begin to work on defining the characteristics of their ideal team. Then they will see how they each stack up against these characteristics that they helped define, and work up an improvement plan for those areas where they've determined they need help.

Towards the end of this work, the staff (and probably the owner/manager as well) will be quite surprised to realise that they have evolved into a high-performance team. And the owner/manager will begin to see that more work is being produced and less rework has to be done.

These participatory staff meetings are only one part of an overall team building initiative. Other areas that are addressed include identifying critical areas of needed company improvement, devising strategies for achieving them, defining short-term and long-term goals for each sector of your business, and finally, developing a plan for continuous, ongoing improvement to avoid slipping back into the old ways of doing things. All of this is done with the goal of developing the full potential of the staff and the business.

TEAM-BUILDING AND COMMUNICATION

For the purposes of the Business English teacher it is useful to note the importance attributed to team-building; and understand the procedures involved in building effective teams. It is also important for the Business English teacher to think about how language and communication can be used in building effective teams.

If we review the steps needed to develop a team, it clear that effective communication is central to the processes involved in:
- achieving the commitment of all team members
- defining the mission and vision of the business and then sharing those definitions with the staff
- sharing the decision-making process with the employees
- running and facilitating participatory staff meetings.

Our role is to train Business English users in the appropriate language and communication tools to accomplish successfully the processes needed to build effective teams.

> ### DISCUSSION
> 1 What type of tasks do you enjoy doing as a member of a team?
> 2 Are teams always better at completing tasks than individuals?
> 3 What is the role of language and communication in effective team building?

DELEGATION

Delegation is part of the repertoire of management skills aimed at increasing a manager's overall effectiveness. It is recognised that no single person can carry out all the functions in today's complex organisations. By delegating tasks to others, managers can achieve more. It is linked to other areas of current interest such as time management, people management and decision-making. In contrast to leadership, delegation is a skill that can (and must be) be learned, if managers are to work effectively in their roles.

International Management Centres define delegation as the act of passing to a person (or position) the whole (or part) of the formal authority and accountability for carrying out specific activities. When delegating, the manager gives authority to the subordinate. The manager gives enough responsibility for the subordinate to perform the task. The subordinate accepts responsibility for the performance of the task but the manager keeps overall responsibility. For this reason, delegation can only be effective if it is linked with a system of control based on known targets and standards so that the manager can assess the results achieved.

Delegation is a contentious area. Few managers like to think that they are bad at this, for poor delegation often means poor managerial ability. Some people take naturally to delegating work, others need to train their delegation skills. Any system of delegation must follow logical concepts and techniques, remembering that there are no simple solutions, only general guidelines. All delegation needs to be carefully planned, but the manager must remember that the test of any management system is whether it works in practice. To produce comprehensive personal planning systems likely to suit all managers' needs is impossible. However, we can draw together the main features needed to utilise the enormous capacity of the human brain. In this way we can obtain maximum results in minimum time, with reduced feelings of stress.

Factors in delegation

Factors in delegation that also apply to the operation of any institution include:
1. Policy – contributing effectively to the objectives of the enterprise.
2. Organisation – providing everyone with work of adequate nature, scope and range.
3. Procedures and techniques – ensuring that each person uses suitable tools or techniques.
4. Technology – making sure that everyone works in an appropriate setting.
5. Leadership effectiveness or motivation; giving everyone a chance to use their own specific skills.

Used properly, delegation can result in:
- the advantages of specialisation
- freedom for the manager
- a defined pattern of responsibilities
- a system of training.

To be effective, delegation demands:
- full passing and acceptance of authority and responsibility
- an accepted and workable system of control
- freedom for the subordinate within their terms of reference
 an environment where everyone accepts the benefits of delegation.

Trust

The key to successful delegation lies in the trust between the manager and the subordinate. Trust relies on:
- mutual confidence in each other's ability, reliability and honesty
- working together to make trust grow
- the acceptance that trust is fragile
- a culture that encourages its growth.

Trust is increased if:
- the manager has some say in picking his subordinate

- the boundaries of the area of delegation are clearly defined
- control is directed towards ends not means
- parameters, objectives and control mechanisms are agreed jointly
- action is the responsibility of the subordinate.

DELEGATION IN PRACTICE

Effective delegation depends on forethought and planning. Because two people are involved, it is necessary to plan in more detail and to use both manager and subordinate in the planning process.

The importance of delegation is recognised in most large organisations by the use of job descriptions. These lay down the tasks to be done and the duties and responsibilities of the person employed. Unfortunately, this loses the idea that delegation is a contract between the manager and the subordinate. A job description can be criticised because:

- it applies to the job not the job holder, taking no account of their personal skills and aptitudes
- it becomes too rigid and does not apply to the everyday operational aspects of the job.

In contrast, delegation can combine flexibility with continuity and not become too rigid.

The need for delegation arises when a position becomes too busy or too complex. The manager tries to reduce the burden on time, energy or personal skills and passes over some of the workload. In all cases, the manager passes on certain duties while keeping overall responsibility. Note that we have used the words manager and subordinate, but that it is also possible for a task to be delegated upwards to a superior, or sideways to a colleague.

Delegation can be considered as a routine, almost inevitable factor associated with growth in size or complexity. In practice it is more complicated. It can be to an individual, a team, a machine or to a system. However it is done, the overall responsibility rests with the manager. The manager is responsible for:

- ensuring that the subordinate is trained, competent and trustworthy
- laying down precise terms and conditions of appointment
- incorporating a system of accountability and control.

DELEGATION TO NON-HUMANS

Even more difficult problems occur when work is delegated to non-humans. Increasingly, computers are taking over aspects of management previously carried out by staff solely responsible to the manager. Now the task is shared between the information provider, the software designer, the computer itself, and the person interpreting the results. In the short term, this means that delegation must be very carefully designed to show the paths of accountability. In the long term, it becomes a matter of organisational change and development.

HOW TO DELEGATE?
Peter Drucker (in *The Effective Executive*) answers this most simply: get rid of anything that can be done by someone else. The main factors that stand in the way of such a simple solution are:
- the delusion that only I can do that task
- a natural reluctance to relinquish any job that you enjoy doing
- the difficulty in accepting that a job can be done satisfactorily by someone with less knowledge, skill or understanding
- lack of understanding that delegation is a means of preparing subordinates for positions of greater responsibility
- not understanding that a task is delegated to a person as well as to a position. When a new subordinate takes up a position, it is essential to review all delegation to match the tasks to the new person
- failing to recognise the true nature of responsibility and accountability in a delegated task
- the subordinate is accountable to the manager who retains overall responsibility to whatever superior authority exists.

STEPS IN DELEGATION
Delegation is not an ad hoc activity to be carried out as and when a manager feels under pressure. To be effective, it needs to be integrated into systematic working procedures and carried out through a series of planned steps. These can be summarised as:
- deciding what to delegate
- deciding who to delegate to
- delegating the task
- establishing a feedback system for information to be transmitted back and forth between all parties involved in the delegated activities.

DELEGATION AND COMMUNICATION
Each of the management skills considered so far in this chapter have been associated with communication. Delegation is no different. At its core are, of course, decisions about what to delegate and who to delegate. However, the conceptual elements involved in the what and who need to be matched by communication skills if the delegation itself is to be effectively communicated. For the Business English teacher, it is useful to note the importance attributed to delegation in large organisations; and to think about the skills required to communicate the delegation and to ensure the feedback system for information is well carried through.

Effective communication is central to the processes involved in:
1 explaining the tasks to the people to whom you are delegating
2 understanding their reservations and concerns

3 getting their agreement and commitment
4 sharing feedback on progress of delegated tasks.

Much of this communication will take place in face-to-face meetings, where the skills necessary for running a meeting will be important in establishing the right climate and dealing with core issues. As with other management skills, our role is to train Business English users in the appropriate language and communication tools to accomplish successfully the processes needed to delegate tasks effectively.

> **DISCUSSION**
> 1 Do you try to delegate certain tasks or do you prefer to do everything yourself?
> 2 Is delegation always the best way to achieve the best results?
> 3 What is the role of language and communication in effective delegation?

6 Communication across Cultures

As we saw in the last chapter, communication is what managers and their teams spend most of their time doing. It is their main tool for carrying out the following management activities:
- leadership in order to inspire and motivate colleagues and subordinates
- team building in order to harness the synergies of individuals brought together from different disciplines and with different specialisations
- delegation which aims to share responsibility, empower subordinates and free up superiors.

However, there is another level at which we can see communication – namely in terms of its role in a cross-cultural environment.

In the second half of the twentieth century, business people have seen their organisations become more complex in two areas. Firstly, in the world of work the range of business knowledge and skills needed to perform effectively has increased. Today's business people are required to be much greater multi-specialists than their forerunners. The neat compartmentalisation which characterised the scientific management approach (see The Evolution of Management in Chapter 2) has been replaced by a complex series of competences in specialist, semi-specialist and generalist areas. Secondly, in the international working environment, business people are much more likely today to find themselves together with others from different national and cultural backgrounds. The internationalisation of the business world, the breakdown of national barriers and the mobility of business people has provided a new challenge for Business English teachers: how to prepare learners for the range of cultural settings in which their learners may be required to use English.

The concept of culture has become a popular topic when talking about companies. At one time, IBM was often quoted as an example of a business culture that transcended national boundaries. As IBM had such power in the high technology marketplace, it was believed that IBM culture was stronger than the national cultures of the countries in which it operated. As IBM expanded its business operations around the world, it set up offices with the characteristic IBM culture in terms of business values, working styles, etc. So, if you were an IBM manager, you would expect to find a familiar business culture throughout IBM offices world-wide. (Since then the company's dominant position in the computer marketplace has been under attack from a whole range of equipment manufacturers and suppliers, and today it has lost much of its business and cultural supremacy). So, what exactly do we mean by culture?

A useful starting point for understanding the scope of culture is the following model. Here each outer layer of the 'onion' impacts on the inner layers, until we reach the individual, who is a product of cultural influences and personality attributes.

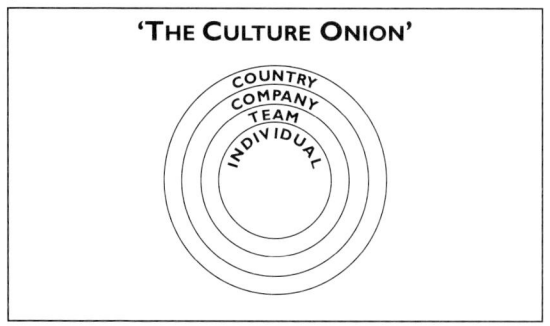

'THE CULTURE ONION'

COUNTRY
COMPANY
TEAM
INDIVIDUAL

The first major influence is national culture, which may be defined as everything relating to a nation's identity, in fact everything that could be considered to have contributed to the present attributes of (a group of) its people. The second is company culture, particularly where a company strives to form and disseminate a set of corporate values, as in the case of IBM above. The third level is team or department. Here we are looking at the specific written or unwritten rules which govern a particular group. For example the finance personnel of many companies see their role in terms of controlling the expenditure of money, and this might be viewed by other departments as a salient cultural feature of the finance department. This may lead to conflict in cases where other freer-spending departments feel that corporate objectives cannot be met because of the difficulty in gaining access to funds for new projects, new products or new strategies.

John Mole, author of *Mind Your Manners*, defines culture simply as ' the way we do things round here'. This is in marked contrast to the long lists of these 'elements of culture' produced by culture scholars to describe in detail where we come from and what has fashioned our thoughts and behaviours. Here are some key categories:

Ideas	Behaviour	Products
beliefs	gestures	literature
values	customs/habits	dress
institutions	language	folklore
		art and music

National characteristics show themselves in many areas of activity and undoubtedly also play a role in shaping company life and culture. So when we refer to business culture, there are a number of visible and invisible features that the members of this culture should share, values that they should subscribe to, norms that they should follow. In an ideal world, the synergistic efforts of the like-minded would encourage everyone to pull together – to the ultimate benefit of the company. In this ideal environment, employees will feel committed and motivated when they can work within the accepted standards and fit into the cultural setting; employees are likely to be ill at ease where they do not feel empathy for the company culture.

Here are some factors which affect national and business culture. Some originate from and are based in the world of work itself; others originate in the local environment and influence the world of work.

Work	Social	Physical
Company organisation	Roles of the sexes	Space between people
The importance of hierarchy	Priorities of personal life	Contact
Attitudes to authority	and work	Handshakes
Respect for leadership	Dress	Gestures
Delegation	Punctuality	Exposure of body
Planning	Ways of addressing others	Facial expressions
Co-operation vs. competition	Openness of conversation	Speech: volume, speed
Team vs. individual	Formality	Acknowledgement of
International attitudes	Taboos	speech
Industrial relations	Humour	Smells
The working day		
Organisation and running		
of meetings		
Company communication:		
– written/spoken		
– tone/style		
Mobility of personnel		

John Mole has produced a template for charting company culture from just two of the above parameters: leadership (from individual to group) and organisation (from organic to systematic). His map of Europe looks like this:

```
INDIVIDUAL
L
E                               FRANCE
A            SPAIN
D                                              USA
E
R       PORTUGAL    BELGIUM
S                                       GERMANY
H                            LUX
I
P              IRELAND
         GREECE              UK         DENMARK
GROUP          ITALY
                                    NETHERLANDS
         ─────────────────────────────────────────
            ORGANIC                 SYSTEMATIC
                    ORGANISATION
```

Culture is not an issue – except where there are conflicts. This is true both in the wider society and in narrower groupings, such as companies, departments or teams. Corporate cultural conflicts can arise in a variety of ways and for a variety of reasons. Firstly, where a company draws its teams from different backgrounds (national or corporate), it is important to establish common ground for members to work together. Where this does not happen, there is the potential for culture conflict and this can, in turn, lead to dysfunctional working. In other words, rather than achieving synergy, the team does not achieve its true potential. Secondly, where a merger, acquisition or joint venture creates a business entity whose management does not share the local culture, national or corporate, there is scope for culture conflict. There are many examples of expatriations of senior managers ending in failure, either because the manager has not been adequately prepared for the 'cultural work setting' or because the family has not been able to adapt to the 'local cultural norms'. Although it is difficult to put a precise figure on it, the costs of these failures are estimated to run into billions of dollars for US companies alone.

The reasons for raising the issue of culture in a book on Teaching Business English are twofold:

1. Business people learning English are likely to have contact across national and cultural borders, both incoming (foreigners moving into their local culture) and outgoing (their own contacts outside their local culture). Thus, they should have some awareness of cultural issues affecting the work and working relationships.
2. Language is embedded in the culture(s) in which it is used. (Some would say that language is a product of culture). Therefore, while teachers of English cannot be expected to know all the minutiae of English-speaking cultures world-wide, some knowledge is going to help their learners become more aware of the behaviours that will help them achieve their business objectives and avoid blunders, both inside and outside the company setting.

The role of the Business English trainer is to teach language and communication. It is not within our core responsibility to teach culture, change behaviour patterns or act as informants about national or corporate cultural values. As with other elements which are extraneous to the central Business English teaching mix, it is important that we are aware of the interrelationship between language, communication and culture. In this way we can help our learners:
- better understand the interrelationship for themselves
- avoid conflicts arising out of the negligent or innocent use of inappropriate language or communication
- avoid the pitfalls that may lead to a dysfunctional working environment.

The York Associates Teaching Business English Handbook

DISCUSSION
1 What patterns of social behaviour are characteristic of your culture? Think about dress, body language, physical contact, the ways of addressing others, openness in conversation, formality, taboos, humour, etc.
2 Using John Mole's parameters, where would you place the business culture in your country?
3 Both culture and personality combine in forming a person. How do you see the balance between the two?

Part Two

Pedagogic Issues for Teaching Business English

7 PRE-COURSE

The pre-course phase is partly administrative and partly pedagogic. It includes all the steps between the student's decision to attend a course and the start date. The period of time may be longer or shorter, depending on a number of prevailing conditions. Courses may be extensive (for example one or two ninety minute lessons per week for twelve weeks) or intensive (for example, a full-time course lasting one or two weeks). For our purposes here, I shall take the intensive course as an efficient model for learning Business English.

Some trainees are able to plan their intensive training well in advance (up to six months before a course starts); for others the decision may be made at very short notice. This may be for a variety of reasons:
1 because a slack time at work allows training to be fitted in
2 an urgent need for training has arisen
3 short-term planning for areas such as training is the norm.

In all cases, it is up to the training organisation to respond with details about the course itself as well as about payment; and, in the case of an intensive course, about travel and accommodation as well. Each organisation will have its own procedures for handling these areas, either through pre-printed material, personalised letters, phone calls or a combination of these.

In this chapter, we will concentrate on the pedagogic pre-course aspects of setting up a Business English course.

NEEDS ANALYSIS AND COURSE OBJECTIVES

Business English belongs pedagogically to ESP, the key to which is the degree of specificity of the course in relation to the students' needs. Specificity can be viewed in a number of different ways:
- the content should be based around the learners' professional background(s)
- the language knowledge (specialist vocabulary) should be drawn from the learners' professional backgrounds
- the communication skills taught should practise the skills needed in the real professional world
- the training style should be adapted to the learners' preferences
- the programme may include content-based training, provided by specialists in professional content, management skill or corporate culture.

These points are not exclusive to the Business English classroom. The General English classroom may also draw on the learners' language background and target skills in developing a teaching programme. However, Business English trainees typically have more precisely defined needs from a course and these needs translate into a more clearly-cut programme.

In order to get the fullest picture of the trainees and their training objectives, it is useful to see the needs analysis stage as consisting of three separate but linked elements:
1. the range of communication and language required in the trainee's present or future professional role
2. the current ability of the trainee in terms of language and communication
3. the actual objectives of the training programme.

Mathematically speaking, the content of the training programme should be based on the formula: $1 - 2 = 3$. However, student needs $(1 - 2)$ do not always equal 3 (actual objectives):

In order to complete this phase, we must firstly address the questions:
- What types of information do we need to get?
- How can we get this information?
- How can we translate the information collected into objectives?

In the earlier chapters, we summarised the scope of Business English in terms of developing language knowledge and developing communication skills. Our needs analysis, therefore, needs to add some substance to these foundations, as shown in the following diagram.

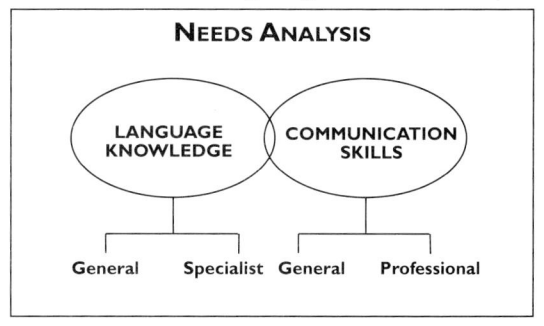

NEEDS ANALYSIS

LANGUAGE KNOWLEDGE — COMMUNICATION SKILLS

General Specialist General Professional

General language knowledge. The range of areas likely to be identified here are:
- extending general purpose vocabulary
- extending topic-based vocabulary, e.g. politics, law and order, social trends, etc.
- enriching range of expression through idioms, synonymy, antonymy, etc.
- extending knowledge of key phrases for social contact
- reviewing core grammar
- extending knowledge of grammar
- correcting grammar mistakes
- improving pronunciation.

Specialist language knowledge. This normally involves extending specialist vocabulary around key professional areas. This may include not only the individual's own area, but also other areas of interest to the trainee.

General communication skills. The range of areas likely to be identified here are:
- developing skills in social communication, including language for travel, restaurants and general social contact. This can include both listening and speaking, and, in some cases, reading documents such as public signs, menus, timetables, etc.
- developing skills for discussion around topics of general interest.

Professional communication skills. This wide range can best be summarised under the heading of the four skills or skill combinations:
Speaking / Listening. The two-way process of communicating and understanding communication in:
- presentations
- meetings – controlling and participating
- negotiations
- interviewing

Listening. Understanding the gist and detail of different types of speech models including:
- native speaker normal speed (colloquial) e.g. general discussion
- native speaker normal speed (formal) e.g. TV news broadcast
- native speaker reduced speed, e.g. ELT audio cassette
- non-native speaker – strongly marked in terms of vocabulary, grammar and pronunciation
- non-native speaker – weakly marked in terms of vocabulary, grammar and pronunciation

Reading. Understanding the gist and detail of different types of texts, including:
- correspondence (letter, fax, memo, e-mail)
- reports
- technical/professional documentation, e.g. contracts, instruction manuals, product descriptions, academic papers, etc.
- realia from the general native speaker world, e.g. public notices, street advertising, etc.
- newspapers, magazines, journals, Internet, etc.

Writing. The ability to produce different types of texts, including:
- correspondence (letter, fax, memo, e-mail)
- reports
- technical/professional documentation, e.g. contracts, instruction manuals, product descriptions, academic papers, etc.

The degree to which these needs are accommodated by the training programme will depend on the course type:

Individual courses. This is, in many ways, the ideal situation for a tailor-made course. Individual training provides the opportunity for the trainee to have a programme customised in terms of content, pace and training approach.

Closed group courses. A closed group should be a more or less homogeneous group of trainees. Closed groups may be composed of individuals from:
- the same company, but from different specialist areas (single company course)
- the same professional function within one company, including its subsidiaries (marketing course)
- the same department (personnel course)
- the same team.

In each of the above situations, there can be a lesser or greater overlap in terms of course objectives and entry levels.

Open group courses. An open group course (sometimes called a public course) may draw its participants from a wide audience. In open Business English or Executive English programmes, the trainees typically come from different geographical, corporate and professional areas. Therefore, such kinds of general Business English programmes need to tread a judicious path in order to satisfy the possibly diverse objectives of the participants.

In terms of satisfying needs, the individual course offers the most straightforward teaching situation and the open group course the most complicated. In order to facilitate the process of satisfying needs, it is important to carry out some kinds of needs analysis. This can be done either pre-course or on the first day. The rigour and detail of any pre-course needs analysis will depend, largely, on systems for collecting data. The following data collection methods require varying levels of human and technical resources:

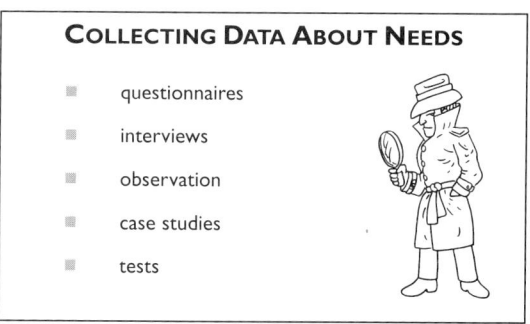

COLLECTING DATA ABOUT NEEDS

- questionnaires
- interviews
- observation
- case studies
- tests

Questionnaires. Most training organisations have some form of registration document which participants complete when enrolling on a course (see below). This can include a questionnaire about objectives for the training programme.

Course Registration Form

PERSONAL

Name:

Nationality:

Mother tongue:

Date of birth:

Company:

Business address:

Telephone: Fax:

E-mail:

Company activity:

PROFESSIONAL

Do you need English for your present job?   YES ☐   NO ☐
your future job?   YES ☐   NO ☐

Your job title:

Principal job activities:

COURSE OBJECTIVES
Please indicate your priorities for your training.(1 highest, 4 lowest):
1. To develop your **general language knowledge**, i.e. general vocabulary and grammar
2. To develop your specialist language knowledge, i.e. vocabulary/expressions in your specialist field
3. To develop your **general communication skills**, i.e. discussion and social contact
4. To develop your **professional communication skills**, i.e. meetings, presentations, telephoning and writing
5. Other:

COURSE REGISTRATION FORM (continued)

Now indicate which areas are important for you to cover, using the following table.

	Priority		
	High	Medium	Low

Speaking
presenting at meetings or conferences
using the telephone
participating in informal meetings (2 - 6 people)
chairing meetings or conferences
participating in negotiations
giving instructions and training
socializing with visitors
other:

Listening
following training courses
understanding discussion at meetings
listening to conference speeches/lectures/etc.
other:

Writing
writing letters / faxes / e-mails
writing reports and minutes
other:

Reading
reading letters / faxes / e-mails
reading journals / magazines / newspapers
other:

Please give any other relevant details here:

COURSE REGISTRATION FORM (continued)

LANGUAGE LEVEL

Please circle the number of the paragraph which best describes your level in English.

9
I use an extensive range of English equivalent to that I use in my own language and suitable for all business occasions

8
I can use a full range of English in all business situations with proficiency approaching that in my own language, with only occasional minor problems.

7
I can use English effectively in most business situations with few problems. My communication in business English is effective and consistent, with few hesitations or uncertainties.

6
I can use English competently in a variety of business situations but with noticeable faults. I can usually communicate effectively in English and, when difficulties arise, communication is restored easily.

5
I can usually communicate my message in most business and social situations. I still have problems saying what I want to say and understanding other people.

4
I can communicate in familiar business and social situations. I make a lot of mistakes and I have problems understanding other people.

3
I can manage simple business communication, e.g. on the telephone and in a meeting, if other people speak slowly and clearly.

2
I can have a simple conversation in English.

1
I can use only a few words of English, e.g. greetings, and I can recognise public notices and signs.

0
I do not understand or speak any English.

Give details of English studies and/or visits to English-speaking countries.

Interviews. A second method of collecting data about needs is through an interview. If the training organisation is locally based, then a member of the pedagogic staff can arrange a face-to-face interview with the prospective trainee(s). If this is not possible, then the interview can be carried out by phone.

The following communication network is derived from a face-to-face interview. It aims to identify:
- who the learner communicates with in English for professional purposes
- how the learner communicates (communication skills)
- what the learner communicates about (professional content)

The starting point is to write the trainee's initials, in this case GS, and his/her job title in the centre of a whiteboard and then to proceed with questions about who, how and what.

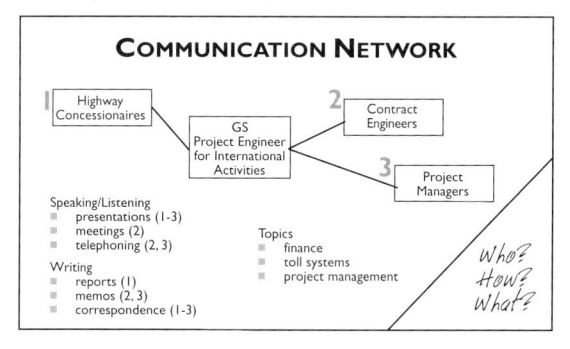

COMMUNICATION NETWORK

1. Highway Concessionaires
2. Contract Engineers
3. Project Managers

GS Project Engineer for International Activities

Speaking/Listening
- presentations (1-3)
- meetings (2)
- telephoning (2, 3)

Writing
- reports (1)
- memos (2, 3)
- correspondence (1-3)

Topics
- finance
- toll systems
- project management

Who? How? What?

Key
- GS are the trainee's initials and his job title is project engineer for international activities.
- 1, 2 and 3 represent his main lines of professional communication in English (who)
- The first column shows the communication skills required with 1, 2 and 3 (how)
- The middle column shows the topic areas or subjects he communicates about (what)

The interview provides not only a method for collecting data about the trainee's needs for English, but also an opportunity for an initial evaluation of language knowledge and communicative ability. However, this type of job description works best where both interviewer and trainee are face-to-face, sharing information written (either by the interviewer or the trainee) on the board. On the phone, without the support of sharing the information on the whiteboard, the job exposition can become a much more complex task for both parties. And if this is their initial contact, it can be daunting and possibly damaging for the training relationship.

A simpler approach for a telephone interview is via the following questions, which aim to provide the interviewer with an overview of the trainee's track record, before moving on to the more complex area of training needs. The information on this form is elicited by interview questions (which can, of course, also be used in a face-to-face interview.)

Interview Assessment

PERSONAL
Name: First name:

Languages spoken:

PROFESSIONAL
The present
Job title:
Department:
Work of department:

Job duties:

English use in present job:

The past. Previous jobs:

The future. Future job plans:

SOCIAL
Hobbies:

COURSE
Course objectives:

INTERVIEWER'S ASSESSMENT

Observation. In some cases it is possible to gain access to trainees' professional environment and observe them at work. Though work-shadowing can provide some first-hand knowledge about the scope of communication needs and present level of competence, the data collected will need to be supplemented by interview in order to complete the communication network. In theory observation represents an attractive method of gaining realistic data; however, in practice it usually presents strategic difficulties in terms of physical and informational access. So, while in-company trainers may occasionally be invited to watch their prospective trainees in action, external training organisations are unlikely to be encouraged to intrude into the work environment.

Observation, however, is not limited to listening to oral communication in action. Where writing is a training priority, trainees can be asked to provide samples of their written work, usually on condition that they are handled confidentially by the training organisation. This can provide a good insight into:
- the types of document to be produced
- the content areas and topics to be covered
- the range and fields of specialist vocabulary
- the current level of writing competence, both linguistic and stylistic.

Case studies. A case study is a detailed, intensive study of an entity, such as a company, a department, a division or a team, that stresses factors which contributed to its success or failure. As such it is mostly commonly used as a group training tool to enhance management knowledge and skills on management training courses. The knowledge and skills gained can later be applied by trainees to their own professional contexts. In the classroom itself, trainees study a case and then explore (either through discussion or in writing) aspects relating to the entity's performance.

The idea of using a case study as an evaluation tool is that it can provide a multi-disciplinary platform that a group of trainees could discuss. During the discussion (and from any follow-up writing), the trainer can collect valuable information about the current level of language knowledge and communication skills. It is a useful device for a number of reasons, the main ones being:
1. it is related to the professional environment, though not specifically to the trainees' own day-to-day experiences
2. it combines within one context a number of professional management areas, enabling trainees with different management backgrounds to contribute to the task
3. it can provide a platform for the full range of communicative tasks and activities, i.e. discussion, presentation, meeting, negotiation, as well as writing, reading and listening.

Tests. There are many types of test formats. They range from the formal right/wrong norm-referenced test paper (grammar and vocabulary) to the less formal better/worse fluency rating based around communicative tasks. All test formats have their role to play in assessing the trainee's level of competence, though it is important to recognise the strengths and limitations of each test type. So, while case studies can be considered a type of test as described above, they typically provide a method for evaluating a wider range of language and communication around management-oriented themes. Formal norm-referenced tests, on the other hand, can best be used to check:
- language knowledge
- listening comprehension
- reading comprehension
- writing skills
- controlled or semi-controlled speaking (in interview with the tester).

So, as data collection instruments, tests are most useful in telling us about the trainee's current of competence rather than his/her present language or communication needs.

At the beginning of this chapter, I stated that the aims of the needs analysis stage are:
- to collect data about the range of communication and language required in the trainee's present or future professional role
- to assess the current ability of the trainee in terms of language and communication.

Having considered a number of methods for carrying out this stage, it is for each training organisation to decide which activities of those listed, either singly or in combination, will yield the most reliable information for course planning purposes.

FROM DATA COLLECTION TO COURSE OBJECTIVES

The data collection itself is not the final stage in needs analysis, as present needs minus present competence does not always equal course objectives. A key feature of ESP courses is the negotiation and agreement on course objectives. Therefore it is important to recognise that the information about present needs and present competence are only inputs into the next stage of agreeing objectives.

On individual courses, the task of agreeing objectives is simple. The trainee is the only customer whose wishes need to be considered. This gives the trainee enormous flexibility in specifying the precise objectives of the course. For example, an individual may want to polish a presentation for a key speech to be given to senior management. If this is the only objective, then the available time can be devoted to getting this absolutely right. Clearly this could not be done with the same intensity and attention to detail in a group course.

Group courses usually involve compromise. As a trainer faced with a

disparate group of individuals, either on an open group course or even on a closed group course, one cannot normally satisfy all the people all the time. Therefore, it is important to:
- explain this to the trainees
- take all of their objectives into account
- reach a negotiated agreement, which aims to satisfy all the people some of the time

The first stage is to collect the objectives. This can be done either by referring to the registration document or by asking them to write down their objectives on a piece of paper. The next stage is for the trainer to transfer this information onto the whiteboard, stressing common themes around the key words of language and communication. By judicious arrangement it is usually possible to summarise the objectives within the main areas of:
- general language knowledge
- specialist language knowledge
- general communication skills (including listening)
- professional communication skills.

Below are some examples of objectives negotiated at the beginning of the course for different types of individual and group programmes. As you will see, the above themes recur regularly, though the phrasing varies according to the trainee's views and expressions.

Objectives for Individual Course for low level learner
- To develop oral skills, especially for presentations and discussions
- To improve knowledge and control of grammar
- To increase specialist vocabulary

Objectives for Individual Course for high level learner
- To develop oral communication skills for general and professional contact
- To improve writing for professional purposes
- To extend general and technical vocabulary
- To improve language knowledge and get feedback on language accuracy, especially grammar and vocabulary

Objectives for a 'Business Communication in English' Open Group Course
- To develop general language knowledge in terms of general grammar, general and business vocabulary and expressions
- To develop specialist language knowledge in the participants' professional areas
- To develop and practise the professional communication skills of meetings, presentations, telephoning, and writing
- To develop and practise general communication skills in order to increase fluency through social language, general discussion and case studies on business issues.

Objectives for an 'Effective Professional Communication for Personnel Managers' Closed Group Course
- To improve professional communication skills in terms of presentations and meetings
- To improve language knowledge in terms of professional and general vocabulary
- To exchange information and opinions in discussions around shared professional issues
- To get feedback on language mistakes.

Objectives for a 'Presentation Skills in English' Closed Group Course
- To develop presentation skills in terms of effective organisation
- To improve presentation techniques in order to have greater impact on the audience
- To learn appropriate expressions for presentations
- To practise presentations and get feedback on strengths and weaknesses
- To review design and exploitation of visual aids.

Course objectives are not written in stone to be slavishly followed throughout the programme. Just as they are negotiated at the beginning of a course, there should be opportunities to renegotiate them at significant points during the programme. Regular feedback sessions are a method for the trainer to involve the trainees in the programme and its direction. This is particularly important on extensive courses and intensive courses of more than about four days, where priorities can change as trainees better understand their own strengths and weaknesses.

> **DISCUSSION**
> 1 What methods do you use to collect data about your trainees' needs? What problems, if any, do you face when collecting data?
> 2 What are the typical needs identified by your trainees?

ASSESSING ENTRY LEVELS

Assessing entry level is important for two reasons. Firstly, it is the mostly widely asked question by trainees: how is my English? Secondly, assessing a trainee's entry level is one of the major prerequisites for course design. Crudely put, course objectives minus current ability should approximate to programme outline. However, it is difficult to find a wholly satisfactory solution as the whole area of assessment is fraught with difficulties due to the absence of a complete set of agreed criteria for scientifically assessing what we are teaching: competence based around accuracy of language knowledge, fluency and effectiveness of communication. Although we can test accuracy-based knowledge, we must depend to a lesser or greater extent on our subjective judgement when it comes to fluency and effectiveness. So, without a coherent framework for measuring competence, all attempts at evaluation must accept a mix of objectivity and subjectivity.

This mix is shown in the following scale, developed by the English Speaking Union, which combines the notions of accuracy, fluency and effectiveness discussed earlier. As a tool, it covers the relevant criteria and is easy to administer and to understand. It can be done as part of the needs analysis during an interview, observation or a case study. The result is that the trainer can quickly give the trainee a score between 0 and 9, representing the entry level. This goes some way to satisfying the trainee's curiosity, as well as providing a user-friendly scale for training managers and others to understand.

In some organisations, a more formal test is carried out to evaluate entry level. This could then be similar to the type of testing procedure described in the earlier section on Needs Analysis. As noted there, tests are one of the repertoire of tools that trainers have to evaluate trainees' competence and are particularly useful if assessing discrete norm-referenced, accuracy-based elements involved in:

- correct use of language forms
- listening comprehension
- reading comprehension
- writing skills
- controlled or semi-controlled speaking (in interview with the tester).

	LANGUAGE PROFICIENCY SCALE
9	Has a full command of the language, tackling the most difficult tasks with consistent accuracy, fluency, appropriate usage, organisation and comprehension. An exceptional level of mastery, not always reached by native speakers, even quite educated ones.
8	Uses a full range of language with proficiency approaching that in the learner's own mother tongue. Copes well even with demanding and complex language situations. Makes occasional minor lapses in accuracy, fluency, appropriacy and organisation which do not affect communication. Only rare uncertainties in conveying or comprehending the content of the message.
7	Uses language effectively in most situations, except the very complex and difficult. A few lapses in accuracy, fluency, appropriacy and organisation, but communication is effective and consistent, with only a few uncertainties in conveying or comprehending the content of the message.

LANGUAGE PROFICIENCY SCALE (continued)

6	Uses the language with confidence in moderately difficult situations. Noticeable lapses in accuracy, fluency, appropriacy and organisation in complex situations, but communication and comprehension are effective on most occasions, and are easily restored when difficulties arise.
5	Uses language independently and effectively in all familiar and moderately difficult situations. Rather frequent lapses in accuracy, fluency, appropriacy and organisation, but usually succeeds in communicating and comprehending general message.
4	Uses basic range of language, sufficient for familiar and non-pressuring situations. Many lapses in accuracy, fluency, appropriacy and organisation, restricting continual communication and comprehension, so frequent efforts are needed to ensure communicative intention is achieved.
3	Uses a limited range of language, sufficient for simple practical needs. In more exacting situations, there are frequent problems in accuracy, fluency, appropriacy and organisation, so that normal communication and comprehension frequently break down or are difficult to keep going.
2	Uses a very narrow range of language, adequate for basic needs and simple situations. Does not really have sufficient language to cope with normal day-to-day, real-life communication, but basic communication is possible with adequate opportunities for assistance. Uses short, often inaccurately and inappropriately worded messages, with constant lapses in fluency.
1	Uses a few words or phrases such as common greetings, and recognises some public notices or signs. At the lowest level, recognises which language is being used.
0	Zero competence

DISCUSSION
1 How do you assess entry levels?
2 Where do the majority of your students fall in the above scale?
3 Are you satisfied with the entry level assessment tool you use? If not, how could it be improved?

Programme Outline and Trainee Briefing

Just as the data collected at the needs stage provide an input into the course objectives, the course objectives are the starting point for agreeing on the programme outline. The aim at this stage is to agree on:
- the length of time to be devoted to each element identified in the objectives
- the types of input and output to be used for each element identified in the objectives
- the ways of working for the group, including the types of training approach to be used by the trainer.

None of these elements are fixed for the course duration and it is important to reconsider them at significant points during the programme.

Length of time for each objective. On individual courses, the trainer can accommodate the trainee's wishes and adapt as the programme develops. For group courses, it is necessary to reach some kind of consensus, taking into account the priorities of the participants. It is equally important for course planning for the trainer to know what proportion of the course is to be devoted to each element.

Inputs and outputs. Inputs refers to the types of material which are to be used in the classroom. These can be either raw materials, such as print, audio or video not developed for the ELT classroom, or published materials, specifically developed for the ELT classroom. Outputs refers to the themes and activities for communication practice. In terms of inputs, trainees may have been asked to bring with them relevant material from their professional area, which can be used as the basis for materials development or lesson development; on the other hand they may rely on the trainer to provide material from the training organisation's resources (either raw or published).

At the programme outline stage, it is useful for the trainer to present the options and agree the types of material and activities to be used in relation to each objective.

Ways of working. This refers to the roles of trainer and trainee(s) and involves:
- how the trainer and trainees will work together to achieve their objectives: the trainees' expectations of the trainer and trainer's expectations of the trainees
- who will be responsible for what in the classroom in terms of preparing inputs and outputs
- what types of preparation/homework are expected outside the classroom.

Pedagogic Issues for Teaching Business English

Trainee briefing. Developing competence in a foreign language requires effort, commitment and discipline. All trainees embarking on a training course want to improve their competence – in terms of accuracy, fluency or effectiveness, or a combination. However many of them have been out of the language learning environment for some time and, despite having a clear idea of their objectives, they may not have reflected on the procedures needed to achieve them. It is therefore useful to spend some time on explaining how to develop competence in a foreign language, the role of study and practice. The following diagram can be used as a starting point to discuss language and communication development.

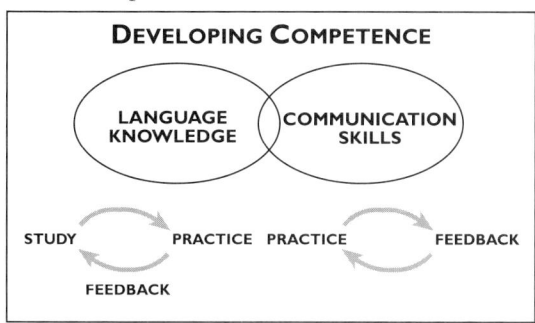

```
          DEVELOPING COMPETENCE

         ┌─────────┐  ┌──────────────┐
         │LANGUAGE │  │COMMUNICATION │
         │KNOWLEDGE│  │    SKILLS    │
         └─────────┘  └──────────────┘
    STUDY      PRACTICE  PRACTICE      FEEDBACK
              FEEDBACK
```

Together the elements considered in these two chapters prepare the groundwork for the course by establishing a set of agreed parameters for programme development. Having reached consensus on these points, the training programme can start.

DISCUSSION
1 Do you include other items in the programme outline?
2 Do you think it is useful or necessary to provide some form of learner training at the beginning of a course?
3 Are there any other elements, not mentioned in this chapter, which should be included in the pre-course phase?

8 On Course

The pre-course phase includes all the steps between the student's decision to attend a course and the start of the course. The on course phase also includes a range of administrative, social and pedagogic areas. Here we will concentrate on the teaching side. However, we should remember that, for intensive courses especially, it is the total package of training, accommodation, social activities and administrative support which lead to customer satisfaction. If one element is unsatisfactory, it is likely to have an impact on the trainee's evaluation of the total package.

In this section, we will concentrate on the pedagogic on-course aspects of running Business English courses. Teaching, of course, covers a wide range of disciplines. I have chosen the following areas, as being of special interest to Business English teachers:
- lesson planning
- learning styles and training styles
- giving feedback
- one-to-one teaching and group teaching.

Planning a lesson

There is no doubt that communicative methodology has revolutionised all areas of ELT, including ESP. Pre-1975, the emphasis of most language teaching was on developing knowledge of the language forms in terms of grammar and vocabulary. Identified through linguistic analysis, these elements were subsequently organised into teaching programmes and course materials. Students learned about the language rather than how to use it. The communicative revolution of the mid-seventies clearly established fluency as the prime objective of language teaching and language training. Out went language drills; in came pair work and small group communicative activities. Thus the communicative approach is one major influence on Business English methodology.

As the scope of Business English also includes communication skills training, classroom practices have also been influenced by approaches derived from other disciplines, including management and communication training. Yet in the attempts to push forward the state of the profession and provide a varied diet for our learners, there is the risk of losing sight of the essential, basic model of learning.

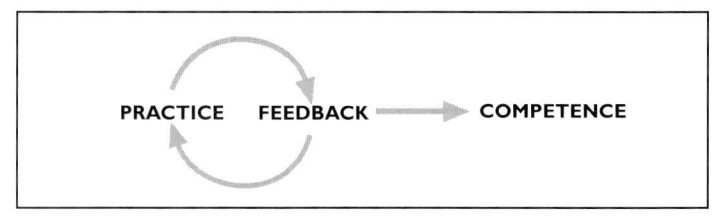

PRACTICE ⇄ FEEDBACK ⟶ COMPETENCE

Thus the feedback loop is central to developing competence, which, hopefully, will result from the practice and feedback provided both inside and outside the classroom. However, this model, though simple, is concerned with learning not with learners, and with training, not with trainers. In this chapter we will explore how this basic model can be translated into a lesson plan. Finally, of course, the dominant influence on training is the trainer's own personal style. However, this point is for the practitioners themselves to consider.

A lesson is a series of interrelated steps which aim to develop an aspect of language knowledge or communication skills, according to the course objectives. Viewed in terms of the global aim of improving competence, it is a small part of a very large whole. However, each lesson should have its own unique aim(s), coherence and outputs.

The following Business English lesson plan presents a flexible model, consisting of up to six stages.

```
                A Classroom Model
    STAGE 1 INPUT TEXT: FOCUS ON CONTENT
     Listening or reading text chosen for its
                informational content
            + task focusing on content
       What text?            What task?
     Oral presentation   Information transfer
         Meeting             Note-taking
     Written report   Comprehension questions
```

```
STAGE 2 FOCUS ON LANGUAGE
Presentation of language points
What points?
Grammar
Vocabulary
Functions
Pronunciation
```

```
STAGE 4 FOCUS ON COMMUNICATION
    Presentation of communication
                         features
              What features?
       Presentation structure
        Presentation delivery
          Controlling meetings
            Letter organisation
```

```
STAGE 3 LANGUAGE PRACTICE
Controlled activities to practise
the points presented at stage 2/4
What exercises?
Gap/fill
Sentence manipulation
Word families
```

```
STAGE 5 COMMUNICATION PRACTICE
                  What tasks?
           Mini-presentations
              Meeting excerpts
     Controlled letter-writing
```

```
       STAGE 6 OUTPUT TASK: PUTTING IT TOGETHER
            A speaking or writing task based around:
          • a communicative† activity to develop fluency, or
          • a communication‡ activity to develop effectiveness
         The context for either activity will be drawn from:
                   • course materials and/or
         • the trainees' own professional or personal experience
```

† a communicative activity is primarily a classroom task designed to activate language and develop fluency
‡ a communication activity is based around a real world skill and is primarily designed to develop effectiveness

Stage 1. This stage provides informational content about a business or professional area. In order to provide focus for the task (a reason for listening or reading), the input text should be accompanied by an appropriate task. The input text used as a model may be either a listening or a reading text. If the objective of the lesson is to develop communication skills, the input text should provide a model for the output task (Stage 6). In other words, a presentation provides a suitable input model for developing presentation skills, a meeting for developing meetings skills, etc.

Stage 2. Whereas the first stage focuses on the informational content of the input text, stage 2 focuses on the language content. This may be a grammatical area, a functional area, key vocabulary or pronunciation patterns. One text may lend itself to different language foci and the teacher will need to decide which focus best meets the students' needs. The trainer's role at this stage is to present, usually at the whiteboard, the key features of the language forms.

Stage 3. While stage 2 is concerned with the presentation of language forms and patterns, at the third stage the student gets an opportunity to practise those forms and patterns through a range of controlled exercises. The aim of the controlled exercise is to focus the trainee's attention on the forms presented and provide an exercise to check the ability to manipulate the forms correctly.

Stages 4 and 5. While stages 2 and 3 focus on the language forms presented in the input text, a parallel operation may be carried out for communication skills, for example presentations, meetings, phoning, interviewing, report-writing, letter-writing, etc. In this way the fourth stage would look at models for a particular mode of communication in order to raise awareness of:
- procedures
- behaviours

as well as
- associated language.

The models can be presented by the trainer him/herself. Where this is impractical, then video or audio models can be used to present the key features. In the same way as stage 2 focuses on the forms and functions of the language, stage 4 analyses the techniques and strategies of communication, as well as associated language. Examples are:

Presentations
- opening a presentation
- linking ideas in a presentation
- summarising and concluding a presentation
- delivering effectively to an international audience in terms of tempo, volume, visual aids, etc.

Meetings
- chairing a meeting
- controlling a meeting
- inviting contributions to a meeting

The elements above are examples of the types of building blocks of communication, parallel in some ways to the grammatical building blocks of language. Once identified, they need to be organised as training elements in a coherent sequence of steps to form a programme of instruction for the communication skill areas of presentations, meetings, negotiations, etc. Just as stage 3 provides controlled practice of the language forms, stage 5 provides controlled practice of the communication strategies and techniques. This can be done by practising elements of the communication skill in order to check that techniques and associated language can be used effectively.

Stage 6. So far stages 2 – 5 have presented and practised language forms and communication strategies. The final stage provides the opportunity for free practice. Where the lesson focus is on language, then the objective of this stage should be to enable the students to use the language forms presented and practised in earlier stages in a free context. Where the lesson focuses on communication, then the aim at this stage is to provide an opportunity for free transfer of the communication techniques presented and practised. To make a smooth transition between the stages, the context for communication should be based on and correspond with the model presented in stage 1. And so the lesson has almost finished. The only element not yet mentioned is feedback – the indispensable element for developing competence. This will be dealt with in later in this chapter.

At the beginning of the chapter, I wrote that I would present a flexible classroom model. So there are two issues to be considered:
- Do the stages need to follow the sequence outlined?
- Are all the stages necessary?

Having experimented with the model over many years and having written a number of Business English course books based around it, it is second nature to me. However, the model is the servant in the teaching process, not the master. Therefore it is up to each trainer to find permutations which work for their own training style and for the learning style of each trainee group. While stage 1 provides a platform from which to develop the lesson, the other stages can be followed in a variety of permutations, for example:

More traditional: Stages 2, 3 and 6
                           Stages 4, 5 and 6
Less traditional: Stages 6, 2 and 3
                           Stages 6, 4 and 5
Other options   Stages 6, 2, 3 and 6
                           Stages 6, 4, 5 and 6

These are by no means all. What is important for the coherence of the lesson plan is to stay within the focus of the lesson – either language or communication. But by not slavishly following the model, both trainer and trainees will benefit from a more varied diet.

> **DISCUSSION**
> 1 To what extent do you plan your lessons? Which stages of your lessons typically require the most planning?
> 2 What factors cause you to change your plan in the classroom?

LEARNING STYLES

The next question is: how far can we apply the model presented in the last chapter to classroom teaching? As we have seen, it is concerned primarily with learning as a process, and not with learners as people. So, it needs to be validated by a model of learner behaviour and then modified in classroom practice. Valuable work in the area of learning styles has been done by the educational scientists, Honey and Mumford. They suggest that each learner has a preferred learning style that he or she brings to a specific task. In their book, *Manual of Learning Styles* (1992), they identify four styles. Using these four learning styles as a starting point, we can identify the following four types of learners and their learning characteristics:

1 The activist learns by doing the task. In the language classroom, these are the learners who enjoy the communicative tasks or the communication practice. They enjoy using the language and experimenting with communication.
2 The theorist learns by understanding the underlying theory. These are the learners who want to know why a particular language form is used in a specific situation or why a particular communication technique is appropriate in a particular setting.
3 The pragmatist learns by practising in a controlled environment. These learners enjoy the security of controlled practice exercises. They often feel that this stage gives them the confidence to use language forms or communication accurately.
4 The reflector learns by watching others doing the task. These learners are likely to feel insecure about their ability to perform in the language. However, in a secure environment they become willing to participate in the range of communicative tasks and communication activities.

So, given a task, such as learning twenty new words in English or improving presentation techniques, each trainee will approach the task with their own preferred learning style. And, as we all know, some learners will be more successful than others. If we can adapt our training style to their learning style, we can go some way to helping them achieve their learning

objectives more effectively. This approach involves:
- identifying and being aware of our trainees' learning styles
- providing classroom tasks adapted to their style.

It is important to point out that the aim of the learning styles approach is not to try to change our learners' preferred learning styles. In any case, it won't work!

Honey and Mumford have devised a questionnaire which identifies an individual's dominant learning style. Although it is a useful analytical tool when dealing with a large number of people whom one doesn't know, in the teaching situation, trainers quickly get to know the trainees and soon reach, by observation, the same conclusions as the questionnaire.

Having identified the dominant learning styles, we can next match up the lesson stages from the previous chapter against learner types above.

Stage 2 and 4. The focus on language forms and communication patterns should appeal to theorists as they fit the new information into existing knowledge.

Stage 3 and 5. This controlled practice should appeal to the pragmatist who likes to test out the practical applications of the forms and techniques presented.

Stage 6. As far as learning style is concerned, this final stage appeals both to the activist and to the reflector, who will benefit from and develop confidence from seeing the activist 'in action'.

Honey and Mumford suggest that the four learner types are equally spread throughout the population. Therefore, if the Business English classroom were drawn from a cross-section of the population, a lesson planned equally around the stages identified in the previous chapter would be an appropriate starting point for lesson development. However, classes are rarely typical and it is by adapting the plan to the learners that trainers can turn the learning-centred plan into a learner-centred one.

The types of adaptation can be:
- to select lesson stages according to preferred learning styles
- to modify the time allocated to lesson stages so that less popular, though important, areas are covered
- to prioritise and order lesson stages according to preferred learning styles.

In this way the trainer can respond flexibly to the learners and their learning styles.

> **DISCUSSION**
> 1 What are the preferred learning styles of the trainees that you teach?
> 2 To what extent can you adapt your training style to your trainees' learning styles?
> 3 Do you find that you have greater problems with some trainees than with others? Which learning style group do they come from?

GIVING FEEDBACK

One way of looking at training is as a closed-loop system based around the following stages:
1 identifying needs
2 designing training programmes (methodology and materials)
3 delivering training
4 evaluating (programme and trainees).

Phase 4 feeds back into stage 1, so that modifications to subsequent programmes can be made. Phase 4 also feeds back into other phases so that the current programme of instruction can be modified and improved in order to maximise the trainees' learning.

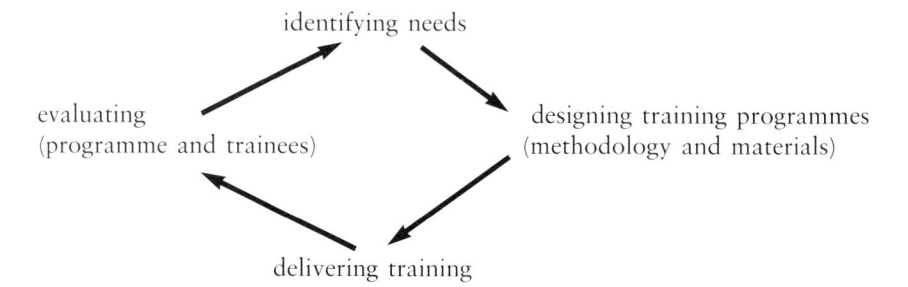

There are three types of evaluation:
1 trainer self-evaluation (you decide how effective your training has been)
2 trainee evaluation (the trainees evaluate how effective the training has been)
3 testing and feedback (the process of determining and communicating to what extent the learning objectives have been achieved)

In this chapter we are concerned with evaluating accuracy, fluency and effectiveness.

Practice and feedback are the essential ingredients in developing competence. And in its widest sense, feedback highlights both strengths and weaknesses, successes and failures. Traditional feedback methods have focused on the accuracy of language forms. However, as we have seen, the

aims of the Business English trainee have grown to encompass other areas of competence, especially fluency of general communication and effectiveness of professional communication; and Business English programmes have followed this lead. As a result, feedback criteria need to reflect this shift. Giving feedback on language accuracy is usually easy, as the use of language forms is normally right or wrong. However, fluency is more problematic. While we all intuitively know what we mean by a fluent speaker and could grade speakers in terms of their fluency, establishing a set of measurable parameters is more difficult. As we have already seen, fluency is:
- flow of speaking
- effort of speaking

while flow is perceived in terms of:
- speed of speaking
- the number of hesitations and pauses.

There are no absolute measurements in terms of words per minute against which we can assess performance, as speakers have their own natural rhythm of speaking, some faster and some slower. So, each speaker's fluency is intuitively assessable according to each listener's own scale of better or worse.

Evaluating effectiveness involves using some right/wrong criteria and some better/worse criteria. Our earlier features of professional effectiveness included:
- impact of communication
- variety of media
- conciseness of communication.

These were subsequently translated into building blocks (procedural, behavioural and linguistic) for the purpose of teaching professional communication skills such as presentations, meeting, negotiations, etc. (see Chapter 4). If we view training as a closed loop system, then these building blocks are both the basis of programme design and the criteria for the evaluation of effectiveness. Two practical examples are shown below:

Presentation Evaluation
Record Of Observations

Note down your comments. Make a note of some words to support your opinion.

STRUCTURE
1. Did the speaker mention what she/he was going to talk about?
2. Did the speaker begin in the audience's area of interest?
3. Was any outline given?
4. Was there a clear development of the speaker's ideas from introduction to conclusion?

DELIVERY - general
5. Did the speaker establish rapport at the beginning of the presentation through:
   a greeting, a smile, eye contact, etc?
6. Did the speaker maintain sufficient eye contact with the audience during the presentation?
7. Did the speaker appear engrossed in his/her message?
8. What was the speaker's manner like? (nervous - unsure - frightened - shy - calm - persuasive - self-confident - superior - arrogant)
9. What was the speaker's body language like? (static - tense - fluid - over-dynamic)
10. Were there any features of the speaker's delivery that you found especially effective?
11. Did the speaker have any mannerisms that you found irritating?
12. Was there enough variety in the presentation to maintain your interest? Consider:
    - variety of tempo, i.e. not all at the same speed
    - variety of volume, including use of pauses and voice modulation
    - variety of sentence structure, especially use of questions, mix of sentence lengths
    - variety of stimuli, such as use of examples, visual aids and other techniques to vary the focus

DELIVERY - specific
13. Do you consider the speaker made a good choice of visual aids?
14. Do you consider that the visual aids were well designed and laid out? Consider:
    - use of graphics
    - use of text
    - size of text and use of fonts
    - use of colours
15. Did the speaker present the visual aids well? Consider:
    - audience contact during presentation of visual aids
    - visibility of visual aids to audience
    - convergence between speaker's words and visual aids

LANGUAGE
16. Was the language understandable in terms of:
    - length of sentences?
    - choice of words?
    - length of pauses?
    - use of link phrases?
    - number of facts per utterance?

OTHER OBSERVATIONS

Meeting Evaluation
Record Of Observations

Note down your comments. Make a note of some words to support your opinion.

PREPARATION
- Have the participants been informed of: date, time, agenda, objectives, specific preparation, documentation, specific roles?

PURPOSE
Do the participants
- share the same expectations?
- have clear objectives?
- understand the scope/limits of the meeting?

PROCEDURE
- Has the procedure (formal chairing, informal brainstorming, etc.) been agreed?
- Has the agenda been agreed and understood?
- Are the time limits clear (duration, finish time, date and time of next meeting)?

ROLES
- Are the roles clearly understood?
- Chairperson - how much control is appropriate?
- Minute-taker - detailed minutes or just a summary?
- Participants - general and/or specific contributions?

COMMUNICATION
- Do all the participants get a chance to contribute?
- Is there a clear direction to the meeting?
- Do the participants understand each other
- Is there a positive atmosphere?
- Is the a clear outcome to the meeting?

LANGUAGE
Was the language understandable in terms of:
- length of sentences
- choice of words
- number of facts per utterance
- length of pauses
- use of link phrases

OTHER OBSERVATIONS

The York Associates Teaching Business English Handbook

We have now fitted evaluation into the closed-loop system of training and provided a coherent approach to evaluating trainee performance in relation to:
- accuracy (traditional categories of correct/incorrect use of language forms)
- effectiveness (performance criteria based around building blocks of effective communication related to specific skills.

We have also noted the difficulty of establishing criteria for evaluating fluency on any measurable scale.

Evaluation should not be a mystery. Just as we negotiate the objectives of the training programmes and the roles that trainer and trainees are to play, we should involve our trainees in the evaluation process. In general terms, feedback should be:
- constructive, i.e. it should not not be used as a stick to beat our trainees with
- balanced, i.e. it should highlight strengths and weaknesses
- transparent so that trainees know what criteria their performance will be judged by
- reasonable so that trainees have a reasonable chance of fulfilling the performance criteria
- shared so that trainees act as evaluators, where appropriate.

In practice, the next stage is to agree with our trainees:
- who will provide the evaluation
- when it will be given
- how it will be given.

THE EVALUATORS

The following chart brings together:
- the range of targets of the Business English classroom
- the types of activities to promote those objectives
- those able to provide evaluation.

TARGETS, ACTIVITIES and EVALUATORS		
TARGETS	ACTIVITIES	EVALUATORS
ACCURACY	STUDY → PRACTICE ← FEEDBACK	TRAINER
FLUENCY	PRACTICE ⇄ FEEDBACK	TRAINEES/ TRAINER
EFFECTIVENESS	PRACTICE ⇄ FEEDBACK	TRAINEES/ TRAINER

1 For accuracy-based tasks, which aim to develop language knowledge, clearly the trainer with his/her superior knowledge of language forms needs to be the evaluator.
2 Fluency, as we have noted above, is about flow of speaking and effort of speaking. Smooth flow is observable (if not measurable), especially over a period of time. In fact, it would be contrary to the normal patterns of fluency development if a foreign language user did not improve just as a result of regular language contact and use. On intensive courses, this is the norm; on extensive courses, it will depend on the frequency of use and contact. In both cases, practice is the key. Thus, fluency develops naturally over time with regular practice, either inside or outside the classroom. With fluency (or perhaps as a result of it) comes increased confidence, which, in turn, brings greater competence: another self-perpetuating closed loop. The better you feel, the better you are. Hence the benefits of alcohol in improving fluency. In the classroom, the smooth flow of language is as apparent to the discerning co-trainees as to the skilled trainer. Therefore all should be encouraged to give feedback on performance. In all cases, it is likely to be subjective. But that is the nature of fluency. Effort, the second parameter of fluency, is in the head of the speaker, not in the ears of the listeners. Only the trainee knows the effort needed to communicate. And, therefore, it is only the trainee who can comment upon this aspect of fluency. Taken together, it is clear that all parties have a role in evaluating fluency: the trainees themselves, fellow trainees and the trainer.
3 Effectiveness of professional communication skills comes from practice. However, as we have seen above, to give programmes a clear focus, they should be constructed around the building blocks of communication. These building blocks are both performance criteria (the objectives of training) and evaluation criteria (the measurements of performance). The question is: who is in a position to comment on performance? Our experience is that the best and most valid results come from involving all parties in the evaluation process. The observation checklists above set the scene and the parameters. All contributors to the communication process (listeners and speakers, presenters and audience, chairperson and participants) should provide their feedback on the effectiveness of communication. Of course, the trainer is in the best position to comment on language.

THE TIMING OF FEEDBACK

The timing of feedback is also a crucial consideration. It can be given during or after the task. Again, the choice will depend on the type of activity and its objective, as well as the range of evaluators involved. During accuracy-based activities, communicative tasks aimed to promote the correct use of language forms, there are some trainees who expressly wish (even demand) instant feedback on their mistakes; others prefer to have a round-up of serious or common mistakes at the end of the activity. As it is the trainer who is responsible for language feedback, he/she will need to reach agreement on this point. Although some learners welcome immediate correction, perceiving this as the true role of the language teacher, the long-term effects on accuracy are often minimal. Mistakes once corrected are, more often than not, repeated systematically in the flow of communication. This is especially true for ingrained errors, which are part of the learner's language system. Ingrained errors are very difficult to eradicate; passing correction does little more than raise momentary awareness. To be effective, persistent errors need to be attacked at source, within the learner's language system. And this can only be done through study and controlled practice of the language forms. So, although on-the-spot correction may give the trainee a sense of learning, the best results are achieved through more serious focus on mistakes after the activity. The feedback is then integrated into the learning process, becoming needs in the four-phase closed-loop training system.

We have noted the problems surrounding feedback on fluency, namely that it will be impressionistic and subjective. In fact, it may be true to say that in some cases the practice itself, the ability to participate in a fluency-based task, such as discussion, is itself a kind of feedback on the trainee's ability to perform a task. Task fulfilment indicates ability; doing is evidence of and feedback on ability. It goes without saying that any feedback on fluency should be handled after the communication practice. Interruptions to give feedback during language use will clearly stop the flow of information or ideas, and may prevent the development of confidence, a key influence on fluency. This may seem a rather laissez-faire approach to training. However, in the range of classroom functions to be carried out by the trainer, the role of orchestrator and facilitator should not be underestimated.

For effectiveness training, based around tasks such as presentations, meetings and negotiations, the feedback can normally only be given after the activity. (The only exception might be where there is a total transgression of a basic rule of communication, leading to a communication breakdown. Here an evaluator may need to intervene with a repair strategy). After the communication practice, notes made during the event, based on observations by all participants, can be used as a starting point for a round table discussion on the successes and failures of communication.

GUIDELINES ON GIVING FEEDBACK
To be effective, feedback needs to be constructive, balanced, transparent and reasonable. These requirements can normally be satisfied by a common-sense approach in terms of techniques. Below are a number of general points to be borne in mind:
1   Practice is, in most cases, more important than feedback. More time

should, therefore, be devoted to practice activities and whatever techniques are chosen, time for feedback should not exceed time for practice.
2. Feedback which involves all the participants, as a team activity, is likely to be more effective than feedback provided by only one person.
3. Feedback which concentrates on negative aspects may undermine learners' confidence. Effective feedback should highlight both strengths and weaknesses.
4. Balance oral and written feedback, according to appropriacy. Remember that some trainees have a better memory of the spoken word; others the written word. Oral feedback through follow-up discussion of communication techniques will usually have greater impact than written notes. On the other hand, written feedback, for example on the whiteboard, on language mistakes will usually be more effective than oral correction.
5. Immediate feedback in more effective than delayed feedback. Provide immediate feedback on effectiveness of communication while the activity is still fresh in the trainees' minds. Language feedback can be provided later for follow-up study, accompanied by practice exercises to focus on language forms.
6. Don't give too much feedback. Base the amount on what you think learners can assimilate from one practice activity or from one lesson. Better a few points that are retained than many that are forgotten.
7. Focus your feedback. If the target is effectiveness, focus your feedback on that area; if accuracy, provide evaluation of language.

DISCUSSION
1. Do you normally discuss with your trainees:
    - the types of feedback you are going to give?
    - the types of feedback your trainees expect?
    - the techniques for giving feedback?
2. To what extent do your trainees normally look to you for feedback? To what extent do they see themselves as evaluators?
3. Do you prefer giving oral or written feedback? Which do your trainees prefer?

ONE-TO-ONE TEACHING AND GROUP TEACHING

No book on Business English would be complete without a section on one-to-one teaching. One-to-one teaching is ESP par excellence, since no other teaching situation offers a greater possibility of programme customisation.

Since the trainee is the sole focus of the trainer's attention, all aspects of the course in terms of objectives, programme design, materials and classroom methodology can be adapted exclusively to the learner's wishes. If every Business English group course is different because of the contributions made by the participants, then every one-to-one course is unique since each individual will stamp their singular mark on the course. And the trainer, of course, is there to respond to those special wishes.

In essence, what differentiates one-to-one training from group training derives from the context itself. One-to-one is individualised and personalised; groups share the trainer and each other. Individual training is single-centred and uniquely focused with the trainer's undivided attention on one person. Group training inevitably calls for compromise on the part of trainer and trainees. From the trainer's point of view, the individual course allows for the greatest flexibility and responsiveness. If the aim of the group course is to satisfy most of the people most of the time, then the aim of the individual course is to satisfy one person all of the time. And that is precisely the reason for the trainee to opt for individual training.

Beyond these essential differences, there are a number of key points which characterise the differences between one-to-one and group training. Some relate to the trainer, some to the trainee and some to the training. However, none of them are absolutes or certainties. None of them are exclusively limited to one course type. They are all features of Business English.

1 **Trainee expectations and trainee behaviour.** Both should have high expectations of the training they are to receive. However, there are normally differences between the two course types. The individual clearly expects a personalised approach and this is what should be delivered. Most group participants, on the other hand, recognise that successful groups need team players. However, some group participants expect more individual attention than is possible. This may be because of their unrealistic expectations or their insensitivity to others. All group participants are individuals, but at the same time they need to recognise that group courses depend for their success on team work. If one person dominates the group, for whatever reason, then the atmosphere suffers.

2 **Trainee involvement and contributions.** Satisfying one person is always easier than satisfying a group. Therefore the individual trainee can be totally involved in all stages of a one-to-one programme – its design and its delivery. The trainee can even direct the programme in a way that would be impossible on a group course. The trainer can freely allow changes of tempo, focus and activity without worrying about the impact this will have. The trainee shares the driving seat and can decide the destination and the speed. Group programmes, however, need to develop a culture of sharing if they are to be successful. Trainees share all aspects of the course, including its design and methodology and individual differences need to be subordinated to the group's wishes if the course is

to be a success. If a single player plays too hard, then the team spirit will suffer. Individual courses provide a unique opportunity for student talk. As the trainee doesn't need to share the floor with other course participants, oral practice time is limited only by the agreement of how trainer and trainee should work together. For the activist learner, seeking the maximum oral practice time, the individual course is ideal. For the theorist, preferring a more analytical and reflective approach to language learning, the constant requirement for the learner to be active may, if not paced correctly, turn into an ordeal.

3 **Trainee level.** Individual courses are best suited to learners who have already attained a certain level of competence and have a clear aim to improve in certain areas. While short bursts of individual training are effective for trainees at all levels, only those who have already attained at least level 4 on the Communicative Competence Scale (see the section in Chapter 7 on Assessing Entry Levels) can truly benefit from the intensity of longer individual training. Lower level learners with fewer linguistic resources and less practice of operating in English will usually tire more quickly than higher level ones with greater language knowledge, communication skills and greater experience of using the language. Individual training should be used carefully with all learners, but particular care should be paid with lower level learners to prevent the experience from overwhelming them and turning the learning experience into a gruelling survival test.

4 **Trainee objectives.** While many of the accuracy- and fluency-based objectives can be developed equally in group and one-to-one courses, there are some communication skills that the individual classroom is not ideally suited for. For trainees who aim to develop their group interaction skills, for example in meetings and negotiations, the individual course is rather limited. Although the trainer can simulate a one-to-one meeting or even role play a group meeting, there are clearly limitations to what can credibly be done to recreate a group meeting with two people.

5 **Trainer approaches.** As we have seen, at the heart of the contrast is the nature of the relationship itself. This leads to a number of key differences in training style. While all training requires both organisation and flexibility, one-to-one training depends on trainer sensitivity to atmospheric shifts in the trainee's mood, attention, interest, etc. Responding to the trainee's personal as well as professional needs and integrating these seamlessly into the training demands a high level of awareness, flexibility and professionalism. Group participants are not well-received when they bring their personal problems into the group arena. Similarly the trainer cannot throw out the planned lesson because one trainee is clearly preoccupied with an extraneous problem which is affecting concentration. Of course, these factors require trainer responsiveness, but it needs to be carried out within the overall plan.

The York Associates Teaching Business English Handbook

Group trainers can adapt, but individual trainers can overhaul.
6 **Trainer characteristics.** For the trainer, running individual programmes requires a particular mix of skills beyond the expertise expected of all ESP teachers. The most important are flexibility and curiosity.
Flexibility affects all parts of the training programme from design to delivery. As each programme is based around the learners and their needs, it follows that each course will be different in certain respects. Trainers need to be able to respond to this variety by designing programmes, each with its own features uniquely adapted to the student. Having designed the outline programme, the trainer will start upon the materials selection phase. Here flexibility is required in choosing, adapting or developing materials which are as relevant as possible to the learner's background. Beyond materials comes the delivery stage, which again needs to be geared to the learner's preferred learning style. In addition, none of these elements – needs, programmes and methodology – are set in stone and trainers are likely to find that as the individual course progresses, changes regularly need to be made to one or more of them. Trainers who can respond flexibly to the fluid situation will find these changes a challenge to their teaching rather than a burden.

Spending between two and six hours a day with one trainee is not everyone's cup of tea. And it must be admitted that not all trainees make ideal companions. However, training is about providing a professional, rather than a social, service and we don't choose our trainers as we do our friends. But the context of individual training naturally brings, or can bring, trainer and trainee close together, usually much closer than in a group course. As a result, the one-to-one situation allows for a wide range of both professional and personal exchanges. This can sometimes even include the unburdening of work and family pressures in the supportive environment of the classroom. While there is a danger that the trainer can become a sponge for all kinds of openness, some of it occasionally unwelcome, the rewards of the experience are in the enrichment that can be gained through the closeness of professional and personal contact. And those trainers with a healthy curiosity of what makes companies and individuals tick are likely to get the greatest personal satisfaction out of one-to-one training.

7 **Training approaches.** As we have seen, at the heart of the contrast is the nature of the relationship itself. This leads to a number of key differences in training style. While all training requires both organisation and flexibility, one-to-one training depends on trainer sensitivity to atmospheric shifts in the trainee's mood, attention, interest, etc. Responding to the trainee's personal as well as professional needs and integrating these seamlessly into the training demands a high level of awareness, flexibility and professionalism. Group participants are not well-received when they bring their personal problems into the group

arena. Similarly the trainer cannot throw out the planned lesson because one trainee is clearly preoccupied with an extraneous problem which is affecting concentration. Of course, these factors require trainer responsiveness, but it needs to be carried out within the overall plan. Group trainers can adapt, but individual trainers can overhaul.

8 **Pacing.** For both the trainer and the trainee, pacing the individual course is critical. Many trainees on short intensive courses immerse themselves so totally in the learning process on day one that by day two they are exhausted or, worse still, saturated. On the other hand, another danger is that trainers, in their eagerness to satisfy all the trainee's wishes on day one, provide such a bewildering array of activities that the trainee leaves the classroom shell-shocked by the unfamiliarity of the learning experience, the intensity of the day and the sheer variety of what has been provided. Therefore, it is good practice for both trainer and trainee to discuss the advantages as well as the pitfalls of individual programmes in the trainee briefing session so that both parties can agree on how to pace the course – certainly one of the most important factors in the course's overall success.

The contexts for group training and one-to-one training are different and this leads to a range of distinctive features at the level of course design and delivery. However, both group training and one-to-one training share many characteristics, based on the commonalities of Business English. Trainers should see that both are ways of delivering a Business English training service within different contexts.

> **DISCUSSION**
> 1 In your experience, what type of trainees benefit most from one-to-one training?
> 2 What do you consider to best the most important attributes of :
>   - a one-to-one trainer?
>   - a group trainer?
> 3 What are the three main differences between materials used on one-to-one course and group courses?
> 4 Which type of training do you (or would you) prefer? Why?

TEACHING OR TRAINING?

Throughout this book, I have used the terms 'teacher' and 'trainer' interchangeably. Although 'teacher' has connotations of school lessons and 'trainer' of professional development, are there any real differences in meaning? Dictionary definitions distinguish between 'teach' and 'train' in the following ways.

Teach
- to impart knowledge or skill
- to provide knowledge of a subject
- to cause to learn by example or experience

Train
- to coach in or accustom to a mode of behaviour or performance
- to make proficient with specialised instruction and practice.

So, "teach" is the most widely applicable term for general education, while "train" suggests concentration on particular skills intended to fit a person for a specific role. As the scope of Business English is both wide and narrow, it would therefore be logical to adopt both terms for the range of activities that we do in the classroom. On the one hand, we aim to help our trainees extend their language knowledge (teaching); on the other to facilitate the development of the communication skills needed in their professional environments (training). In both cases, the learning and practice in the classroom are not an end in themselves – they should act as a bridge to the real world in which language is used as a tool for communication.

Throughout this book, I have particularly highlighted:
- the wide ranging content of Business English with influences drawn from a range of disciplines, including ELT and management training
- the needs-driven approach at the heart of Business English, which requires trainer responsiveness in terms of both content and methodology.

It is, therefore, not surprising that the repertoire of different training styles which trainers may call upon draws on a range of approaches from different areas. In any case, even without the diversity of content which characterises Business English, teaching is a complex area and this chapter can only touch on some key issues relevant to the Business English classroom, in particular:
- the classroom as bridge
- sharing control
- preferred training styles.

THE CLASSROOM AS BRIDGE

There are different types of bridges: some suspended from above, some supported from below. The Business English classroom can also be seen as a bridge, but there are different methods of perceiving and constructing this bridge.

The classroom is, by its nature, a very different place from the real world which most professionals inhabit. In addition, the majority of trainers are, by virtue of their background and philosophy, quite remote from the real world concerns of the business community. If the classroom is to act as a bridge and prepare trainees for the types of communication that they are likely to encounter in the real world, then trainees need to:
- understand something of the business environment

Pedagogic Issues for Teaching Business English

- include activities which prepare trainees for this real world.

The earlier chapters on the business environment, communication skills and management skills have explored these issues from a real world perspective. So, how can they be integrated into the classroom?

The following reflect the diverse viewpoints that trainers may have about the classroom. Each then lends itself to a particular range of activities:
- the classroom should, as far as possible, replicate the real world
- the classroom should develop skills which can be transferred to the real world
- the classroom should provide an environment from which skills will grow naturally
- the classroom should concentrate on helping students acquire a good foundation of language which they can use in the real world.

While in each case the classroom is seen as a bridge to the real world, training approaches and activities will vary according to the views held.

In the real world approach, the trainer will try to recreate in the classroom a believable professional environment through simulations in which trainees will play their own real-life roles. Not only will they be expected to work on their communication skills, but the contexts in which the skills will be practised will aim to simulate professional reality. This may give the classroom a slightly harder edge than the cosy pedagogic norm, but, on the other hand, it can facilitate the development of appropriate skills for use outside the classroom.

Where the classroom is seen as an arena for developing skills for later transfer, the focus will be on practice around case studies, situations which present a reality, but not the trainees' own. These case studies will provide a backdrop against which communication skills can be practised and developed. However, by merging the professional world with the pedagogic world, the trainer can create an arena and environment which encourages feedback along harder lines, sharing with participants the evaluation of performance against professional as well as educational criteria.

For some trainers and some trainees (as well as some lessons), the best results may be achieved by creating an environment where skills can be encouraged to develop naturally. Here, a supportive environment which promotes stress-free learning is the aim. Naturally, tasks can be challenging, but they should be firmly positioned within the ambit of the classroom. Beyond the classroom is another world with its own patterns of behaviour and the trainer's role is to prepare trainees for the demands of this world, but without getting too close to it.

In the final approach, the classroom is seen as separate and divorced from the professional world. This is a less obvious bridge, since the trainees will need to make the jump themselves from the classroom. Here, trainers see their role in terms of giving their trainees a secure linguistic base. A good education will stand them in good stead; and a good grasp of language forms will give them the foundation they require to succeed in the real professional world.

These viewpoints are not mutually exclusive. Trainers, in their training, may move between all of them, adapting teaching methodology according to:
- the learners
- their objectives
- their preferred learning styles.

SHARING CONTROL

The programme of instruction can be divided into a number of linked stages or units, such as a learning module or a classroom lesson. And each larger unit could be further divided into a number of moves. Each move is characterised by an activity, on a cline between trainer-controlled at one extreme and trainee-controlled at the other. The notion of control in the classroom is based around the exercise of direction over the proceedings. Under the strict control of the trainer, the lesson stage follows the content and tempo decided by the trainer, without any possible digression from the planned route. As we move towards a more central position, the trainer allows more and more involvement of and contributions from the trainees. To the right of the central point, the trainees exercise their control over proceedings – initially with the trainer and later with a greater degree of independence, as they move towards recreating the real world.

This illustration highlights the two polarities, but also shows the possibility of many intermediate teaching positions – each corresponding to a different methodological approach. The classroom polarities are shown below.

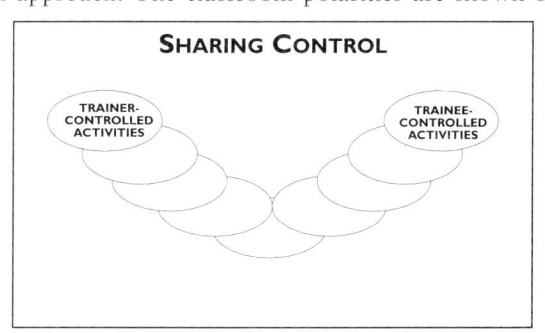

SHARING CONTROL

TRAINER-CONTROLLED ACTIVITIES .... TRAINEE-CONTROLLED ACTIVITIES

Classroom activities or lesson stages also lend themselves to different roles. So, the trainer needs to establish a good correspondence between role and activity. For example, the presentation stage of a lesson where the teacher is explaining a language point or a communication feature is best done in one of the 'trainer-controlled modes'; on the other hand, the transfer stage, involving a communicative activity or communication skill practice, is best done in one of the 'trainee-controlled modes'. The relationship between

Pedagogic Issues for Teaching Business English

TYPES OF CLASSROOM

TRAINER CONTROLLED | **TRAINEE CONTROLLED**

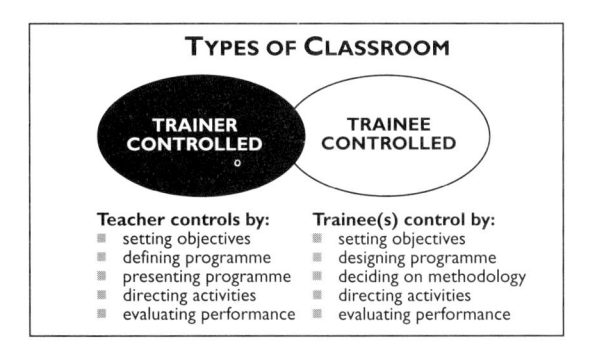

Teacher controls by:
- setting objectives
- defining programme
- presenting programme
- directing activities
- evaluating performance

Trainee(s) control by:
- setting objectives
- designing programme
- deciding on methodology
- directing activities
- evaluating performance

trainer role and classroom activities in shown below. Here language controlled activities are best done in a trainer-controlled mode, communicative and communication activities in a trainee-controlled mode.

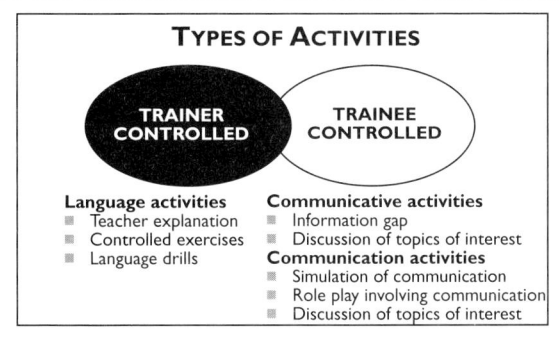

TYPES OF ACTIVITIES

TRAINER CONTROLLED | **TRAINEE CONTROLLED**

Language activities
- Teacher explanation
- Controlled exercises
- Language drills

Communicative activities
- Information gap
- Discussion of topics of interest

Communication activities
- Simulation of communication
- Role play involving communication
- Discussion of topics of interest

Of course, communicative and communication activities can be done in trainer-controlled mode, but then they are less likely to achieve the objectives of increased fluency and effectiveness. The bridge to the real world is best built within a free classroom environment in which trainees are encouraged and allowed to develop their own techniques and strategies.

TRAINING STYLES

Earlier, we explored the mix of learning styles that trainees will bring with them to a learning task, in our case language learning. As trainers, we also have our own preferred training style. However, in our role as provider, our own preferred training approach(es) may need to be subordinated to our trainees' favoured learning mode(s).

Valuable work in the area of training styles has been done by Marshall and Wheeler. They suggest that each trainer has a preferred training style that he or she brings to a specific task and identify four such styles:

1   The listener:

- prefers that trainees talk more than the trainer
- wants learners to be self-directed and autonomous
- appears relaxed and unhurried

2 The director
- takes charge
- gives directions
- appears self-confident
- is well organised
- is the final judge of what is learned
- tells participants what to do

3 The interpreter
- separates self from learners and observes
- uses theory as foundation
- presents well-constructed interpretations
- wants trainees to have a thorough understanding of facts and terminology
- encourages learners to think independently
- provides information based on objective data

4 The coach
- allows learners to evaluate their own progress
- involves trainees in activities and discussions
- draws on the strengths of the group
- uses trainees as resources
- acts as facilitator to make the experience more comfortable and meaningful
- is clearly in charge
- uses activities, projects and problems based on real life.

Beyond the training styles are the many other roles that trainers are expected to fulfil:
- planner
- motivator
- role model
- expert
- follower
- leader
- friend
- human being and even ...
- ... learner

The key to effective training is undoubtedly our flexibility. Although it is important that we are aware of our own preferred style, we must be able to

adapt it to the needs of our learners according to:
- their overall objectives
- their preferred learning styles
- specific lesson targets
- specific features determined by the current environment, such as the time of day, the mood of the learners, etc.

> **DISCUSSION**
> 1 How do you regard yourself in the Business English classroom? As a teacher or as a trainer?
> 2 On the cline from trainer-controlled to trainee-controlled activities, which approach are you most comfortable with?
> 3 Which is your preferred training style?

THE SCOPE OF MATERIALS AND EQUIPMENT

Materials includes all stimuli used as part of a training course to:
- develop knowledge of business and management content
- develop knowledge of language forms
- practise skills of communication.

As such, they can include:
- inputs which stimulate the learner and facilitate the learning process, such as audio, video or written material around business themes
- reference material to be studied and learnt, such as notes on language forms or communication techniques
- practice material to check on the assimilation of new language knowledge or communication skills.

Much of the training material covered during the course will be carefully stored away by the trainees but rarely, if ever, looked at again once the course finishes. Only the accumulated knowledge and skills that the trainee takes from the classroom into the real world is the true legacy of the training programme. Materials, therefore, are only a means to the end of extending knowledge and skills; and equipment is the technical means by which training materials can be activated. Yet the trainer is expected to keep a sharp eye on the range of available resources and their utilisation, remaining up-to-date with published ELT materials and maintaining an informed interest in other areas relating to communication and content.

RAW VERSUS PUBLISHED MATERIALS

Materials for the classroom come in many forms. One basic division can be made between raw materials and published materials. The idea of raw materials is that these have not been specifically adapted for the language classroom. They may be in a form for specialist consumption, such as technical documentation, or in a form for generalist consumption, such as off-air news broadcasts.

As no materials, neither published nor raw, are ever ideally suited to a learner group, the trainer will usually need to spend time on some form of modification or customisation. In the case of published materials, the lesson plan may include part of a unit drawn from published materials, with follow-up activities adapted to the learners' own needs or interests. Raw materials present a specific challenge for the trainer, since they will usually need some degree of effort (and ingenuity) to be useable in the classroom. This may include designing tasks:

- to check understanding of content
- to focus on language
- to focus on communication.

In addition, especially with lower level learners, the trainer may need to pay particular attention to the language level to avoid the 'turn off' experienced by many learners when faced with authentic spoken or written language.

So, the dilemma for the trainer is to balance the pros and cons of published and raw materials in terms of:

- relevance to learners' objectives
- quality of materials as training tools
- the time needed for customisation or adaptation
- cost (the purchase of published materials versus. the customisation of raw materials).

Materials serve a teaching/learning purpose. Therefore neither raw nor published materials are intrinsically better. It is their suitability for the task, according to the above criteria, that determines the final choice. In reality, the Business English trainer is likely to draw from many sources – some published ELT and other raw. More than anything else, a diet from a variety of sources is likely to be more stimulating that from a single source.

FEATURES OF MATERIALS

While suitability remains the overriding consideration in the choice of materials, other factors then play a role in the trainer's selection.

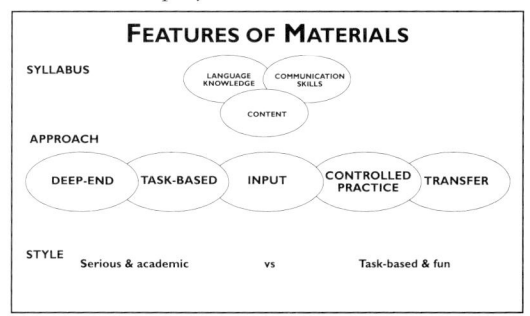

FEATURES OF MATERIALS

SYLLABUS
- LANGUAGE KNOWLEDGE
- COMMUNICATION SKILLS
- CONTENT

APPROACH
- DEEP-END
- TASK-BASED
- INPUT
- CONTROLLED PRACTICE
- TRANSFER

STYLE
Serious & academic   vs   Task-based & fun

Some trainers and trainees see materials as part of a syllabus, an underlying systemic framework on which a teaching strategy is founded. (Thus the grammatical syllabus takes the language, identifies the grammatical units, and reassembles these building blocks into a learning programme). One approach to Business English syllabus design could, therefore, be based on:
- identifying the elements that constitute the scope of Business English
- selecting materials that fit within the syllabus template.

Here, then, the materials are chosen according to the parameters of the syllabus – reflecting the core elements of language, communication and content. At the heart of this choice are considerations of what the materials are. Some are for grammar; others are for communication; and yet others are for content.

A second approach moves away from the notion of syllabus, with its formalised characteristics, to classroom activities. Here materials are chosen, not according to what they are, but rather for what they do; and trainers select for the approach that lends itself best to their trainees' specific learning objectives. Approach-driven materials may be:
- deep end – typically authentic video, audio or text materials which the trainees are expected to handle without preparation; they are thrown into the deep end
- task-based – typically authentic material around which a task has been constructed
- input – material to raise awareness of and teach language forms, communication features, or informational content
- controlled practice – material to check understanding of language forms, communication features, or informational content
- transfer – platform material to lead into a communicative activity or communication activity

Beyond the organisational principles of syllabus and the practical focus of activity comes style. Style includes features such as layout, variety of design, use of colour and overall user-friendliness. Trainee expectations are important here – some will expect a serious, academic style (dense text, few graphics, no colour); others will want a more lively, fun-based style of presentation and activity.

THE MEDIUM OF MATERIALS

The traditional classroom was a place where the teacher, unaided, imparted and shared his/her unique knowledge with learners. As the world has become more complex, the sources of knowledge more diverse, no one trainer can possibly be the fount of all wisdom. However, we are no longer all alone in our role as trainers as we are able to bring parts of the outside world to the classroom.

Beyond the trainer's 'chalk and talk' and the trainees' language and communication practice are a range of materials in different media, which help the trainer to turn the classroom into a varied learning/teaching environment. While printed text remains the most common training medium, today's sophisticated trainees expect teaching media to bring more dynamic and authentic models of language, communication and content into the classroom. Both the ELT world and the non-ELT world give us access to a wide range of video and audio material, and increasingly multimedia. Yet the diversity and availability of materials should not blind us to their real aim – to promote knowledge and learning in the classroom. Therefore we should certainly embrace the new offerings from the publishing houses and other sources. However, we must keep our eye firmly on the suitability of materials for particular learning aims, which are highlighted in the table below.

THE MEDIUM OF MATERIALS		
MEDIUM	**COMPOSITION**	**USE**
PRINT	text / graphics / visual	practice / self-study / reference
VIDEO	slice of life / documentary	input / demonstration
AUDIO	slice of life / documentary	input / demonstration
MULTI-MEDIA	text / graphics / slice of life documentary	all applications

EQUIPMENT

Materials are the software or courseware of training; and equipment is the hardware. To be useable the hardware needs to satisfy certain criteria:
- reliability – it must work first time every time
- ease of use – it must be useable by trainer and trainee without specialist instruction
- accessibility – it must be easy to get to
- utility – it must provide a useful adjunct to the traditional teacher and learner activities.

The reasons why audio is the most common device in the classroom is because:
- it satisfies all the above criteria more completely than other equipment
- it is comparatively cheap to buy and maintain
- it offers more Business English training materials.

Video is catching up on audio in popularity because of the greater impact achieved by combining sound and picture in the learning experience. While video is certainly a very attractive medium for showing longer stretches, there are still issues of ease of use when searching for and replaying short extracts. In addition, published ELT video materials, because of their high production costs and relatively low sales, are still expensive in comparison with cassettes.

The latest addition to the repertoire of equipment is the personal computer (PC). The computer, more than any other device, has revolutionised the way work is done. The computer is also beginning to make its mark in the classroom. The impressive power of the computer, its storage capacity and its tireless repetition of tasks makes it an ideal workhorse. Yet the current crop of machines are bedevilled by problems of complexity and reliability. This will undoubtedly change and we can expect the multimedia experience, harnessing together text, sound and video together on one machine, to become a very attractive teaching and learning tool.

Finally, the humble telephone line is now opening up sophisticated means of distance learning. Telephone teaching (usually regular 30 minute lessons) has taken off in some parts of the world as a practical way for busy executives to maintain their language level. Video-conferencing and videophones offer the potential to deliver distance learning with even greater impact. E-mail is being developed as a possible medium for feedback on written work and the Internet offers the trainer almost limitless sources of topical and authentic material.

DISCUSSION
1 What types of materials do you use?
2 Which sources do you use?
3 What medium of materials do you prefer?
4 Which equipment do you use in the classroom?

9 END OF COURSE

The end-of-course phase, like the pre-course phase, is partly pedagogic and partly administrative. It includes all the steps between the formal end of the training programme and the closing of the trainee's file. The range of procedures should include:
- a course review by the trainees and trainee feedback
- completing the written record of work covered.

In addition, for intensive courses, the training organisation may need to:
- arrange travel and accommodation for the returning trainee
- chase up unpaid invoices
- file away course and trainee documentation

In this chapter, we will concentrate on two areas: review procedures, and course reports.

ENDING THE COURSE

As the course draws to a close, the trainer and the trainee(s) will normally want to complete the cycle that began with the needs analysis and the programme outline. For the trainees it is important:
- to put their recent learning experience into context
- to make some plans for their future learning
- to get some final feedback on their exit level.

Feedback on the trainees' satisfaction with the course is also important for the trainer. Therefore, some method of trainee evaluation should be carried out and the results conveyed to the trainer(s) who worked on the course.

We addressed the subject of level earlier, both in relation to entry and to giving feedback, and noted that all areas of assessment are linked to the perennial questions surrounding accuracy, fluency and effectiveness. In the next section on drafting course reports, we will look again at assessing levels, this time at the end of the course.

An intensive course can be compared to a heavy, but highly nutritious, meal. During an individual or group programme, trainees are taken out of their normal work environment and put into a less familiar environment, where they may struggle to reactivate learning skills long unused. It may be many years since they last studied language; they may be unaccustomed to using the language for such long periods of time. Trainees may find themselves very tired at the end of the training day and perhaps even a little disoriented by the array of new knowledge and skills they have been exposed to. The end-of-course procedures should, therefore, include a look at the past (key areas covered linked to the course objectives); and a look into the future (guidelines for what to do next).

LOOKING AT THE PAST
Training is a closed loop based around the stages of:
- identifying needs
- designing training programmes (methodology and materials)
- delivering training
- evaluating (programme and trainees).

The most appropriate moment for the historical overview is at the very end of stage 3 and just before stage 4. (This does not, of course, preclude the trainer from running regular reviews at the end of each day or even each lesson to focus on what has been covered). It is not intended as a course evaluation, but as a memory refresher, best carried out as an oral session led by the trainer. The aim is to show the trainees the link between their needs and the course content by getting them to stand back from the detail and putting the complete course into context. To run this session effectively, the trainer needs two written records:
1. The objectives that were agreed by the individual or group at the needs analysis/course objectives stage
2. An outline of the main areas covered in terms of language and/or communication.

It is, therefore, essential to keep the record of the initial objectives, together with subsequent modifications agreed with the trainees. This represents their expectations, what they asked for from the course. This needs to be compared with the actual content of the course that was delivered. For this the trainer should synthesise the main elements or modules that the course has covered, writing down on the whiteboard, flipchart or a transparency a summary of the key areas covered, drawing together from the many inputs and outputs the key threads and rationales for those activities. Of course, what the second document should show is a close correspondence with the first document.

LOOKING TO THE FUTURE
As we have noted throughout this book, competence in a foreign language requires a mix of accuracy, fluency and effectiveness. At the pre-course stages we have highlighted these three areas as possible targets for improvement. Now we need to refer back to them and provide guidelines as to how trainees can continue with their learning. In summary:
- developing accuracy of language knowledge is a long-term process requiring regular work on targeted areas of grammar and vocabulary
- developing fluency of general communication requires regular practice to maintain the level of facility acquired through language use during the training programme
- developing effectiveness of professional communication requires practice and feedback on the key features of professional communication.

Developing accuracy can be continued in two learning modes: in the

classroom or through self-study (or a combination of the two). In general, to be effective, accuracy-based training needs to be:
- **regular.** Two hours every week is much more effective than one day a month since the former maintains regular patterns of study leading to better retention and easier recall of language forms;
- **systematic.** The training should aim to build up the learner's language system as a series of linked elements. New areas should be related to old ones as the learner builds up an overall picture of the interconnected linguistic elements. The language forms chosen for learning should not be randomly selected, but should be coherently positioned within the overall linguistic system;
- **focused.** The training should have a clear focus so that trainees know what they are working on and why. For the purposes of increasing language knowledge, it is better to work on a clearly identified small area than try and attack the whole language at once;
- **realistic.** The aims and objectives of learning should be realistically attainable within a short period of time. Motivation comes and continues from seeing one's efforts rewarded by success. Taking small manageable bites is more satisfying than large indigestible ones.

Beyond this, trainees should be encouraged to develop their own learning plans in terms of the time and resources (material and human) available. Obviously, working with a trainer can help to maintain continuous, regular learning practice. Though for many this may be luxury that the demands of work or budget do not permit. However, the market is now very well supplied with a wide range of learning materials, catering for diverse training needs and interests. These can be used in combination with other inputs such as radio, TV and non-ELT published material to provide a motivating mix of learning stimuli around which trainees can prepare their own learning plans, such as the following:

SAMPLE SELF-STUDY PROGRAMMES

INTRODUCTION
Becoming proficient in a foreign language is a long-term process. It requires regular and systematic work in order to achieve specific objectives. This 'work' consists of two elements: study and practice. Study is necessary to learn the grammar and vocabulary of the language. Practice is necessary to develop your communication skills.

LANGUAGE STUDY
Below are some suggestions for the steps to follow.
1   Decide what areas of language you want or need to study. For example, you may decide that you'd like to review the tenses in English; alternatively you might like to look at modal

verbs; or you might like to extend your vocabulary, either in your professional area or around general topics.
2   Make your plan and fix your objectives. Remember that your plan must be realistic and your objectives realisable. It is no use planning to learn 500 new words in a week – or even in a month. Your plan should not only specify your learning targets, but also the time that you plan to devote to achieving your goals. Remember it is better to spend a little time regularly than long periods irregularly.
3   Find some suitable learning materials that will help you to achieve your objectives. (Trainers should recommend their own preferred self-study materials).

Model plan for language study

Objectives:
- to review English tense system
- to learn ten new words per week

Available time:
Two hours per week for ten weeks, based on half an hour per language study session four times a week

---

COMMUNICATION PRACTICE

Developing communication skills requires a systematic and regular approach, just like developing language knowledge. However, there is one key difference. While developing language knowledge requires study, developing communication skills requires practice. The basic rule is: the more you practise, the better you'll get.
1   To start with, you will need to make some decisions about the skills you are interested in developing. At the first level, the choice covers the following:
- listening
- speaking
- reading
- writing

However, within each of the above skills, there are a number of sub-skills. For example, speaking includes:
- presentations
- meetings
- telephoning

In addition, some skills provide a useful platform for language study. For example, articles that you read can provide a rich source of:
- new vocabulary
- examples of key grammar areas.

2   Make your plan and fix your objectives.
3   While language study requires good learning materials, communication practice requires opportunities to make active contact with the language – through speaking, listening, reading and writing.

3.1 Developing speaking skills. Your job may provide you with opportunities for speaking practice. If it does not, or it does not give you enough, then you'll need to look for other possibilities, either by joining a course or by forming an informal practice group among colleagues or friends. (If your aim is to improve your presentation skills, you can do this by yourself with a cassette recorder onto which you record your presentation).

However, before joining or forming a group, make sure that you have agreed with the trainer or other members what the objectives of the group are. In other words, a general conversation class will help you to develop your general fluency, but it won't automatically help you to improve your telephone techniques. The basic rule is: the more you practise your targeted sub-skill, the better you'll get.

3.2 Developing listening skills. There is a wide range of authentic listening material that you have access to via the radio and TV. Suggested TV sources include:
- UK Gold
- Sky
- CNN – mostly American English models

Suggested radio sources include:
- BBC World Service – mostly British English models.

3.3 Developing reading skills. There is a wide range of authentic reading material that you have access to. This includes reading for information as well as reading for pleasure. Suggested sources of reading for information include:
- Daily British or American newspapers
- Magazines such as *Time*, *Newsweek*, *The Economist*, etc.
- English-language publications produced by your company
- Suggested sources of reading for pleasure include: "readers" – simplified literary and popular works at various levels of difficulty, available from ELT bookshops and distributors.

When reading, remember that books provide a rich source of vocabulary and can be used to develop your language knowledge.

3.4 Developing writing skills. Your job may provide you with opportunities for writing practice. If it does not, or it does not give you enough, then you will need to look for ways of improving – either by yourself, based on models, or by joining a course. As with speaking, before joining a group, make sure that you have agreed with the trainer what the objectives of the group are. (Trainers should recommend their own preferred self-study materials).

> **Model plan for communication practice**
> **Objectives:**
> - to practise general conversation
> - to improve listening skills
> - to read for pleasure
>
> **Available time:** 2.5 hours per week for ten weeks.
> **Methodology**
> 1. General conversation
> 45-minute lunch-time meeting once a week with colleagues in the company restaurant, during which only English is spoken.
> 2. Listening skills
> - 15 minutes listening to UK Gold twice a week
> - 10 minutes listening to CNN twice a week
> 3. Reading skills
> 20 minutes spent reading for pleasure twice a week + 15 minutes to write up new words into a special notebook for vocabulary and to review them regularly.

DEVELOPING FLUENCY

Developing fluency of oral communication requires practice. The more one practises, the better one gets. Confidence and competence are interlinked elements in the fluency development process. In terms of follow-up activities, this means that every opportunity to use the language will help trainees maintain the level of fluency achieved during a course. The obverse is also true: lack of practice will lead to loss of fluency over time.

Fluency practice can be provided in two ways: either through real-world language use or through classroom practice. In general, to be effective, fluency-based practice needs to be:

- **Regular.** Two hours every week is much more effective than one day a month since the former maintains regular patterns of use leading to better facility in the language;
- **Wide-ranging and challenging.** The fluency practice should encourage the language user to talk about real issues, encouraging true communication about professional or personal interests rather than controlled practice of language formulae;
- **Based around oral activation.** Developing fluency requires speaking, not study. Therefore it is not achievable within the context of self-study.

This type of practice is topic-driven. It does not require training materials, simply an opportunity and a context. As we have noted, fluency practice is its own feedback. No formal procedures are required. Therefore, the most important elements in fluency development are:
- an interlocutor
- a topic
- plenty of chances to speak.

DEVELOPING EFFECTIVENESS

Effectiveness lies somewhere between accuracy and fluency. On the one hand, it requires practice; on the other it requires feedback. Although some aspects of communication (awareness raising and limited practice) can be developed in self-study mode, the main thrust will need to be based around practice.

Effectiveness development can be provided in two ways: either through real-world language use or through classroom training. However, as we have noted above, to be effective, the practice communication needs to be accompanied by feedback. While the real world can provide plenty of opportunities for practice, this is rarely followed by feedback on the effectiveness of communication. It therefore lacks an essential element.

In general, to be effective, effectiveness-based practice needs to be:
- **Focused.** The communication practice should have a clear focus so that the resulting feedback is meaningful in relation to specific aspects or building blocks of the communication skill being practised. For the purposes of improving a specific communication skill, it is better to work on a clearly identified small area than try and attack the whole skill at once
- **Based around oral activation.** Developing effectiveness requires a mix of awareness raising and communication practice. Although the first area can be approached through self-study, the second cannot.

Just as fluency practice is topic-driven, effectiveness practice is skill-driven. It does not require training materials, simply contexts drawn from the trainee's own personal or professional experience.

The reason for looking into the future is to give the trainees some guidelines about how to continue their learning and what they can realistically do in order to further develop their knowledge and skills. Many leave a Business English with every good intention of continuing to work on the English. The reality is that the pressures of work usually prevent these aims from being fulfilled, except within the contexts of the language requirements of the trainees' jobs.

DISCUSSION
1 How do you end a course? What procedures (administrative or pedagogic) do you need to complete?
2 In your experience, to what extent do your trainees continue to work on their English? What types of activities do they do?
3 What types of follow-up would make your courses more effective?

REVIEWING THE COURSE

The closed-loop system of training consists of the following four phases:
- identifying needs
- designing training programmes (methodology and materials)
- delivering training
- evaluating (programme and trainees).

Programme evaluation should be an ongoing process, as the trainer collects feedback from the trainees and integrates it into other phases of the course – its design and implementation. For the final evaluation, the trainer is getting feedback on the total process and all the elements that have made up the learners' experiences. Broadly speaking, the final course review should focus on:
- the link between phase 1 and the subsequent phases
- the materials used in the training process
- the methodology used by the trainer
- the effectiveness of the trainer him/herself
- the results of the training.

The final review of an intensive course may also want to look at other elements of the total training package such as:
- accommodation (where students have attended a course away from home)
- the social programme
- the training centre's facilities
- the training centre's atmosphere
- the support from the training organisation's administrative staff.

Although these elements are not central to the course itself, they have a direct influence on overall customer satisfaction. Lack of quality in one of these areas can easily lead to dissatisfaction with the whole service, including the training course. It is, therefore, important that training organisations pay attention to their ancillary services.

The course evaluation can be carried out in a number of ways:
1. by the trainer orally
2. by an impartial member of the training organisation orally
3. by a written feedback questionnaire.

For each method the feedback can be based around open evaluation or closed scales, either numerical (1 – 5) or judgmental (very good – very poor). In order to focus the trainees' attention on the key issues, it is useful to have some form of questionnaire as a guide. Below are three models, showing different ways of running the end-of-course review.

ORAL FEEDBACK – OPEN EVALUATION – LED BY TRAINER

In this method, trainees are presented with the questions below by the trainer – on transparency, flipchart or whiteboard. They are told to discuss these between themselves and formulate their conclusions. One person, the spokesperson, will then present the group's consensus to the trainer. During the discussion phase, the trainer leaves the room so that the trainees can deliberate in private. With groups of around six participants, the whole process can be completed in 30 minutes – about half of the time for internal discussion and the other half for presentation of results.

FEEDBACK QUESTIONS

A   How do you evaluate the course in terms of:
   1 Materials
   2 Teaching approaches
   3 Activities (variety and usefulness)
   4 Pace
   5 Level
   6 Appropriacy to needs/interests

B   To what extend do you feel that you have achieved your objectives?

C   Any other comments?

ORAL FEEDBACK – CLOSED-SCALE EVALUATION – LED BY REVIEWER

There are advantages and disadvantages in bringing an outsider into the evaluation process. The greatest benefit is that it brings a degree of objectivity and impartiality into the process which may encourage the trainees to be more truthful and open about their course than if they have to give their feedback to the trainee. In this method, a reviewer, either another trainer whom the trainees know, a pedagogic co-ordinator or the director of studies, runs the evaluation session. The trainees are guided by the following questions, which they answer in advance of the face-to-face meeting with the reviewer. At the meeting the reviewer collects their oral feedback and makes appropriate written notes of the participants' assessments. With groups of around six participants, the whole process can be completed in 30 minutes – about 10 minutes to complete the questionnaire and 20 minutes for the reviewer to guide the assessment session and make notes.

COURSE EVALUATION

Please fill in this form. It will help us to improve the quality of our service.
The co-ordinator will discuss your feedback with you at .... (time) on .... (day).

Student Name:
Company:
Host family/hotel:

Please will you rate the following on a 1 to 5 scale by circling the relevant number where applicable:
1   bad
2   not very good
3   satisfactory
4   good
5   excellent

Please write your comments on any of these points on the other side of this sheet.

1   YOUR COURSE

General assessment	1	2	3	4	5
Objectives clear?	1	2	3	4	5
Objectives followed?	1	2	3	4	5
Contents of course	1	2	3	4	5
Balance between different parts of course programme	1	2	3	4	5
Pace: too fast / too slow?	1	2	3	4	5
Level of difficulty	1	2	3	4	5
Trainer 1 (name:)	1	2	3	4	5
Trainer 2 (name:)	1	2	3	4	5
Your course materials:	1	2	3	4	5

(course file, photocopied material, etc.)

2   OTHER FACTORS

Pre-course administration	1	2	3	4	5
Pre-course materials:	1	2	3	4	5
Administration during your course	1	2	3	4	5
Your accommodation (host family/hotel)	1	2	3	4	5
The training centre	1	2	3	4	5
Lunch arrangements	1	2	3	4	5
The social programme	1	2	3	4	5

3   YOUR COMMENTS

4   HOW CAN WE IMPROVE THE SERVICE WE PROVIDE?

THANK YOU

WRITTEN FEEDBACK – CLOSED-SCALE EVALUATION

There are three reasons why a formal written evaluation may be preferred:
- individual feedback can be given anonymously
- individual feedback can be given quickly
- a formal written record of individual feedback is produced.

Therefore, the written feedback questionnaire is very useful when:
- dealing with large group sizes where discussion may be difficult to organise and consensus difficult to achieve
- either the training organisation or the client needs a written record

The following questionnaire is based around a 1 – 5 rating scale. While other ranges are possible, an odd number is generally considered better than an even number and a smaller number is usually better than a bigger one. Psychologically a five-point scale correlates with:

1 very good
2 good
3 acceptable
4 poor
5 very poor

In some cultures, these values are reversed so that 5 is the highest grade and 1 the lowest.

This questionnaire is used at the end of a general Business English course aiming to develop:
- general language knowledge
- specialist language knowledge
- general communication skills
- professional communication skills.

It can be easily modified to reflect the design of other more specialised Business English programmes.

COURSE EVALUATION FOR LANGUAGE SEMINAR

Please answer the following questions by giving marks from 1 (very weak) to 5 (very good)

1   Course Design
1.1 How do you rate the general language knowledge component and materials?   1 ☐ 2 ☐ 3 ☐ 4 ☐ 5 ☐
1.2 How do you rate the specialist language knowledge component and materials?   1 ☐ 2 ☐ 3 ☐ 4 ☐ 5 ☐
1.3 How do you rate the professional communication skills components and materials?   1 ☐ 2 ☐ 3 ☐ 4 ☐ 5 ☐
1.4 Overall, were you happy with the course?   1 ☐ 2 ☐ 3 ☐ 4 ☐ 5 ☐

2   The Groups
2.1 How do you evaluate the group size? 1 ☐ 2 ☐ 3 ☐ 4 ☐ 5 ☐
2.2 Were the groups homogeneous enough from the point of view of language level?   1 ☐ 2 ☐ 3 ☐ 4 ☐ 5 ☐

3   The Training
3.1 How do you rate the trainers?   1 ☐ 2 ☐ 3 ☐ 4 ☐ 5 ☐
3.2 Did the course move at the right pace?   1 ☐ 2 ☐ 3 ☐ 4 ☐ 5 ☐
3.3 How do you rate the variety of the course activities?   1 ☐ 2 ☐ 3 ☐ 4 ☐ 5 ☐
3.4 How do you rate the usefulness of the above activities?   1 ☐ 2 ☐ 3 ☐ 4 ☐ 5 ☐
3.5 Overall, did the course meet your objectives?   1 ☐ 2 ☐ 3 ☐ 4 ☐ 5 ☐

4   Administration
4.1 Was the course efficiently administrated?   1 ☐ 2 ☐ 3 ☐ 4 ☐ 5 ☐
4.2 Was the social programme satisfactory?   1 ☐ 2 ☐ 3 ☐ 4 ☐ 5 ☐

5   Criticism *
5.1 Are there any ways in which this course could be changed for the better?
5.2 Which part of the course has disappointed you most?
5.3 Which part of the course have you enjoyed most?

6   Other*
Are there any other comments you would like to give in relation to this seminar?

Thank you very much.

(*Author's note: ample space is provided here for the respondent's answers to the questions in sections 5 and 6.)

Whichever method of evaluation is used, the dual objectives of the process should be remembered:
- to collect the trainees' feedback on their satisfaction with the service they have received
- to feed this information back to those responsible for the service so that remedial action can be taken, where necessary

This means that the training organisation will needs systems for transmitting the data to those involved in and responsible for key areas. In the front line are the trainers themselves and where the feedback has been collected by a reviewer, the information that is relevant to the trainers should be passed on to them. Other areas, such as feedback on:
- accommodation (where students have attended a course away from home)
- the social programme
- the training centre's facilities
- the training centre's atmosphere
- the support from the training organisation's administrative staff

should be passed on to the appropriate department

Feedback has been a key issue throughout this book, particularly for the trainees in the learning process. However, it is equally important for the training organisation to have its own feedback procedures so that it can constantly monitor and improve the quality of the service it provides.

> **DISCUSSION**
> 1 How do you collect feedback at the end of a course? What areas do you collect feedback on?
> 2 To what extent are your trainees truthful when giving feedback?
> 3 How could you improve the feedback procedures that you use?

DRAFTING THE COURSE REPORT

The course report provides a framework in which the following elements can be fitted:
- a restatement of the course objectives
- a summary of the course content
- an evaluation of the trainee's achievements
- recommendations for the future.

The course report itself may go to a number of different people:
- the trainee him/herself
- the trainee's boss

- the trainee's training or personnel department.

As the report is a window on the training organisation, it is important that it is:
- well-designed
- well-presented
- meaningful to insiders (the trainee, the training department)
- comprehensible to non-specialists (non-training personnel).

As the report is also an administrative/pedagogic it is important that it is:
- coherent
- comprehensible
- complete.

While much of the report will be based around the past facts (what was agreed in terms of objectives and what was done in terms of course content and activities) and future guidelines (recommendations for follow-up), the report needs to include some form of evaluation of trainee performance. As we have seen in earlier chapters, the whole area of formalised, objective evaluation presents a major challenge, especially where course objectives have included fluency and effectiveness training. This is accentuated at the report drafting stage, when more rigorous assessment procedures and scales are required. The two main problems the report drafter faces are:

1 Simple evaluation scales do not capture adequately the various parameters involved in accuracy, fluency and effectiveness; and complex evaluation scales are only comprehensible to specialists.
2 The trainee is very likely to have improved in certain areas; but the degree of improvement may not be clearly measurable or meaningfully communicable on the scale provided.

While it is good publicity for the training organisation to be able to show the trainee's improvement on a measurable scale, they may have to settle for a more oblique method, as in the following report model which evaluates the trainee's performance according in relation to the course objectives.

The model below follows a simple pattern. It is divided into three sections:
1 the preliminaries
2 the course content
3 comments and recommendations.

MODEL 1: INDIVIDUAL COURSE REPORT

Course Report

Student: A
Client: B
Course type: Individual intensive
Dates: 16 - 20 October 1995
Job:
A is a Deputy Director of B, responsible for the construction of new buildings. He is just about to complete the construction of a new microelectronics factory in C. As from January 1998, he will be in D, working as leader of the project group in charge of the construction of a new B plant in E.
In this project, he will initially need to communicate in English in:
- presentations
- meetings and discussions

with:
- the local council
- the Area Business Park developers
- the Construction Management group
- architects, engineers and contractors working on the project

Entry Profile: Communication Competence level 3
A has a basic, but limited, knowledge of core grammatical forms; his active vocabulary is very restricted; his passive vocabulary, especially of technical and semi-technical terms, is wider.
In terms of speaking, A can express ideas and information in carefully controlled situations with basic accuracy and limited fluency; his listening skills are better and he is able to extract the gist from more complex listening passages; acceptable pronunciation.

Course Objectives:
1 To develop oral skills, especially for presentations and discussions;
2 To improve knowledge and control of grammar;
3 To increase specialist vocabulary.

[Note: The Entry Profile: is based on the ESU Communicative Competence Scale]

Course Content:
1 Oral skills
Presentations and discussion
- introducing the organisation of the project
- stages of project
- the clean room
- the Dresden project

General
- daily routines
- current projects
- past activities
- hobbies and lifestyle
- family and work life

2 Grammar areas
The present simple and present continuous
The past simple and present perfect
Future reference

Individual Course Report (continued)

3 Vocabulary development
General purpose vocabulary
General business vocabulary
Specific construction and project vocabulary
In addition, the daily classroom notes on cassette provided feedback on language accuracy and language style.

[Note: Course content: takes each objective as a subsection heading and describes key areas covered.]

Comments:
A began the course with a rudimentary knowledge of language forms, but with a commitment to gaining the maximum benefit from his two weeks in York. He has worked hard on developing his language knowledge (grammar and vocabulary) and communication skills (presentations and discussions) in English.

1 Oral skills
His oral communication is well-structured, which gives his interlocutors an opportunity to understand the gist and detail of the information. He is able to deliver ideas in a clear and coherent manner, considering the limited means at his disposal.

2 Grammar areas
He has now covered the core grammar verb forms (past, present and future) and can use these with basic accuracy.

3 Vocabulary development
He has a basic working knowledge of vocabulary, which, when used creatively, enables him to express fairly complex ideas.
In general, he needs much more language to operate comfortably and effectively in his new project, but these two weeks have shown him that achieving a working knowledge of English is within his grasp.

Recommendations
Developing a basic working knowledge of a foreign language takes time, and A has already made some progress along that path. In general, to develop his competence still further, he needs practice, feedback and study. Practice and feedback, in order to improve his fluency and professional communication skills; study, in order to consolidate and extend his language knowledge.
In particular he needs to:
- review the grammar covered during the course, using the self-study materials purchased
- extend his grammar and vocabulary, if possible with a trainer to give him feedback on the accuracy of his language
- practise the communication skills of presentations and discussions, again, if possible, with a trainer to give him feedback on the effectiveness of his communication.

Nick Brieger, Training Consultant

[Notes: Comments: takes each objective as a subsection heading and describes performance and improvement achieved during the course.
Recommendations: general paragraph on developing competence followed by specific recommendations in relation to course objectives not yet achieved.]

MODEL 2: GROUP COURSE REPORT

Course Report

Students: Student names and their company names
Course: Business Communication in English
Dates: 19th February – 1st March 1995
Objectives:
- To develop general language knowledge in terms of general grammar, general and business vocabulary and expressions
- To develop specialist language knowledge in the participants' professional areas
- To develop and practise the professional communication skills of presentations, meetings, telephoning, and writing
- To develop and practise general communication skills in order to increase fluency through social language, general discussion and case studies on business issues

Course Content:
General language knowledge
The present tenses
The past tense vs the present perfect
Future reference
Conditionals
In addition, the daily TV news was used to develop listening skills

Specialist language knowledge
Topics covered:
- company organisation
- marketing
- personnel
- finance

Professional communication skills
The following skills were practised during the course:
- presentations
- negotiation
- meetings
- telephoning
- writing

General communication skills
Topic areas included:
- social language for different social contexts
- the environment
- entertainment
- business cultures
- politics
- law and order
- food and drink
- travel

[Note on Course Content: takes each objective as a subsection heading and describes key areas covered]

GROUP COURSE REPORT (CONTINUED)

General assessment:
Language learning is a long-term process, but in the course of these two weeks, everyone in the group achieved greater fluency and confidence in using English, an improved awareness of their errors and enhanced their listening skills. Although there was some difference in language level, the group worked well together and each participant made progress in terms of developing language knowledge, improving communication skills or both.

Nick Brieger and Ann Barker
Training Consultants

SAMPLE INDIVIDUAL ASSESSMENT

Individual Assessment
(Participant) A

Entry Profile: Communicative Competence Level 7 (see attached sheet)
A has a good knowledge of core grammatical forms and vocabulary, both general and technical from her specialist area. In terms of communication, she can express her ideas with reasonable fluency and effectiveness in professional situations; acceptable pronunciation.

Comments
A participated actively throughout the course. She is a competent user of the language, as she demonstrated in her presentation and is comfortable in meetings and discussions.
Her contributions throughout the course demonstrated that she is quite fluent in English. However, she should now consider how to make herself more effective, especially in professional communication.

1 General language knowledge
   A now has a better grasp of the main verb forms in English and an increased understanding of her own weaknesses.
2 Specialist language knowledge
   A has a very good overall knowledge of the language forms from her specialist area together with an extensive repertoire of general business vocabulary.
3 Professional communication skills
   In general A is an effective communicator who is able to use a wide range of techniques which enhance the impact of her message in presentations, meetings and on the phone. During the feedback sessions, we identified a number of areas in which she could improve her overall performance, especially question handling, body language and active listening.

All in all, A has shown that she is able to communicate comfortably with people from different backgrounds (both professional and national) and she should be pleased with the progress made during the course.

Sample Individual Assessment (continued)

```
Recommendations
Developing competence in a foreign language is a long-term
process, and A has already made good progress along that path. In
general, to develop her competence still further, she needs prac-
tice, feedback and study.
Specific areas for A are:
•   effectiveness of professional communication
•   extension of language knowledge
For the former the key is continued practice, with special empha-
sis focus on communication techniques. For the latter, A should
find ways of systematically increasing her active vocabulary. This
could be through reading or listening to English - but with an
ear not only for the message but also for the forms of language
used. This heightened awareness should help her to increase her
language knowledge.
```

[Notes: General Assessment: general statement about the group, their performance and the task of developing competence in a foreign language
Individual Assessment: takes each objective as a subsection heading and describes performance and improvement achieved during the course
Recommendations: general paragraph on developing competence followed by specific recommendations in relation to course objectives not yet achieved.]

No course report can ever paint the whole picture. Therefore it should aim to strike a balance by being:
- complete without being oververbose
- comprehensible without being overcomplex.

Discussion
1 Why do you think that a training organisation should prepare a report on each trainee?
2 What information should the report include?
3 For which audience should the report be written?

PART 3 THREE

CHECKLISTS

These checklists are not intended to be exhaustive. The intention is rather to give a basic selection of references which you can use as a basis for further development yourself.
In spite of attempts to avoid information which is likely to go out of date quickly, some of the references will inevitably change. York Associates hopes in the future to be able to provide updated information via its website.
British telephone and fax numbers are given with the local code only. If calling from abroad, dial the national code 44 and then the local code without the first zero.

CHECKLIST 1
FURTHER READING

This is a basic reading list for newcomers to the subject of teaching Business English.

BOOKS
Ellis, M. and Johnson, C. (1994). *Teaching Business English*. Oxford: Oxford University Press.
Hutchinson, T. and Waters, A. (1987). *English for Specific Purposes - A Learning-centred Approach*. Cambridge: Cambridge University Press.
Robinson, P. (1990). *ESP Today*. Hemel Hempstead: Prentice Hall.
Wilberg, P. (1987). *One to One*. Sussex: Language Teaching Publications.

REPORTS
Dudley-Evans, A. and St John, M. J. (1996). *Report on Business English: A Review of Research and Published Teaching Materials*. Princeton: Educational Testing Services.

JOURNALS
Language and Intercultural Training, published by Language Training Services, focuses on language training for companies, available from LTS, 5 Belvedere, Lansdown Road, Bath, Avon BA1 5ED, UK.

Checklist 2

Professional Development for Teachers of Business English

Professional associations

The main professional association outside the United States is IATEFL - the International Association of Teachers of English as a Foreign Language. Individual members can also join any of a growing number of SIGs - Special Interest Groups. The must for practising and aspiring BE teachers is the biggest SIG, BESIG, the Business English Special Interest Group, which organises its own annual international conference - usually in Germany in November - and publishes its own newsletter. Contact: IATEFL, 3 Kingsdown Chambers, Kingsdown Park, Whitstable, Kent CT5 2DJ, UK. Tel: 01227 276528, Fax: 01227 274415, E-mail: 100070.1327@compuserve.com
BESIG also produces resources indexes from time to time: the last one appeared in 1993.
The Management and Computer SIGs also organise seminars and produce informative newsletters.
The other (US-based) international professional organisation is TESOL - Teachers of English to Speakers of Other Languages: 1600 Cameron Street, Suite 300, Alexandria, VA 22314-2751, USA.

Professional press

The EL Gazette, published monthly, contains news and reviews of interest to BE as well as to General EFL teachers. Available from 5th floor, Dilke House, 1 Malet Street, London WC1 7JA, tel: 0171 255 1969, fax: 0171 255 1972, e-mail: 100130.2037@compuserve.com

Job and career information

The EL Gazette publishes a regular jobs supplement: *EL Prospects* which contains profiles on pay and conditions in different parts of the world as well as job advertisements.
The ELT Guide, published annually and available from the same address, offers useful general advice on both jobs and qualifications.
As well as a job information exchange centre at its annual conference, IATEFL runs an electronic jobshop on the World Wide Web at http://www.go-ed.com/jobs/iatefl/

Qualifications

The best qualification for general EFL teachers who want to have an initial qualification in BET is the LCCI (London Chamber of Commerce and Industry) Certificate in Teaching Business English. Contact: York Associates, 116 Micklegate, York YO1 1JY or the LCCI Examinations Board, 112

Station Road, Sidcup, Kent DA15 7BJ, tel: 0181 302 0261, fax: 0181 309 5169 / 302 4169.

PROFESSIONAL DEVELOPMENT
Why not:
- form a Business English Teachers' development group in your area?
- write an article for a BET magazine - or start a magazine yourself?
- make a proposal for a presentation at the next teachers' conference you can get to?
- write some training materials and circulate them to colleagues for piloting?
- contact the author with comments, questions or requests for help?

CHECKLIST 3

PUBLISHED MATERIALS FOR TEACHING ENGLISH

The trickle of Business English materials in the seventies and early eighties has now turned into a mighty flood and, if possible, you should have a regular browse through the new titles in a specialist ELT bookshop or at a publishers' exhibition at an ELT conference.

PUBLISHERS
Write to the major BE publishers to go on their mailing lists for their annual catalogues and news of new publications. The big three are:
Cambridge University Press, The Edinburgh Building, Shaftesbury Road, Cambridge CB2 2RU. Tel: 01223 325846, fax: 01223 325984, e-mail: eltmail@cup.cam.ac.uk
Longman Group Ltd., Longman House, Burnt Mill, Harlow, Essex CM20 2JE, tel: 01279 623623 / 426721, fax: 01279 431059.
Oxford University Press, ELT Division, Great Clarendon Street, Oxford OX2 6DP. Tel: 01865 267567, fax: 01865 267831, e-mail: elt.enquiry@oup.co.uk, World Wide Web http://www.oup.co.uk/elt

Also notable for BE titles are:
Collins Cobuild, HarperCollins Publishers, 77-85 Fulham Palace Road, Hammersmith, London W6 8JB. Tel: 0181 741 7070 Fax: 0181 307 4629 internet: http://www.cobuild.collins.co.uk
Heinemann, Heinemann English Language Teaching, Halley Court, Jordan Hill, Oxford OX2 8EJ. Tel: 01865 311366 Fax: 01865 314193.
e-mail: helt@bhein.rel.co.uk

internet: http://www.heinemann.co.uk
Language Teaching Publications, 35 Church Road, Hove BN3 2BE. Tel: 01273 736344, fax: 01273 720898.
Penguin English, 27 Wrights Lane, London W8 5TZ. Tel: 0171 416 3000, fax: 0171 416 3060.
Peter Collin Publishing (for specialist dictionaries), 1 Cambridge Road, Teddington, Middlesex, TW11 8DT. Tel: 0181 943 3386, fax: 0181 943 1673, e-mail: info@pcp.co.uk
Prentice Hall / Phoenix, Campus 400, Maylands Avenue, Hemel Hempstead, Herts HP2 7EZ, tel: 01442 881900, fax: 01442 882151.

Books

This list is a selection of the books published mainly over the last ten years which would collectively form a good basis to a Business English teaching resources centre. For ease of reference, the titles are given first. The classification is imperfect since some titles do not fit easily into one single category.

Coursebooks

Advanced Business Contacts. Nick Brieger and Jeremy Comfort. Prentice Hall 1994.
Business Basics. David Grant and Robert McLarty. OUP 1995.
Business Challenges. Nina O'Driscoll and Fiona Scott Barrett. Longman 1996.
Business Class. David Cotton and Sue Robbins. Nelson 1993.
Business Connections. M. Carrier and M. Sneyd. Longman 1992.
Business English. Peter Wilberg and Michael Lewis. LTP 1990.
Business Matters. Mark Powell. LTP 1996.
Business Objectives. Vicki Hollett. OUP 1992.
Business Opportunities. Vicki Hollett. OUP 1994.
Business Review. Kay Bruce, Betsy Parrish, Allan Wood. Longman 1992.
Business Venture. Roger Barnard and Jeff Cady. OUP 1993.
Developing Business Contacts. Nick Brieger and Jeremy Comfort. Prentice Hall 1993.
Early Business Contacts. Nick Brieger and Jeremy Comfort. Prentice Hall 1994.
English for Business Communication. Simon Sweeney. CUP 1997.
English Works. Robert O'Neill. Longman 1993.
Executive Decisions. A. G. Fowles et al. Longman 1995.
Functioning in Business. P. Lance Knowles, Francis Bailey, Rosi Jillett. Longman 1991.
Getting Ahead. Sarah Jones-Macziola and Greg White. CUP 1993.
Going Places. Gillian Porter-Ladousse. Heinemann 1995.
International Express. Liz Taylor. OUP 1996.
Multilevel Business English Programme. Ian Badger and Pete Menzies. Macmillan 1993.
New International Business English. Leo Jones and Richard Alexander. CUP 1996.
People in Business. Michael Kleindl and David Pickles. Longman Business English 1992.
Professional English. Mark Ellis, Nina O'Driscoll and Adrian Pilbeam. Longman 1984.

Language
Build Your Business Grammar. T. Bowen. LTP 1996.
Business Idioms International. C. Goddard. Prentice Hall 1994.
Business Language Practice. John Morrison Milne. LTP 1994.
Early Language of Business English. Nick Brieger and Simon Sweeney. Prentice Hall 1997.
Language of Business English. Nick Brieger and Simon Sweeney. Prentice Hall 1994.
Language of Business English Workbook. Nick Brieger and Simon Sweeney. Prentice Hall 1996.

Listening
Business Listening Tasks. Patrick Hanks and Jim Corbett. CUP 1986.
Business Talk. Gareth Hughes, Adrian Pilbeam and Christine West. Longman 1982.
Executive Listening. Ed. Mark Waistell. Nelson 1993.
Make or Break. David Evans. BBC Publications 1992.
Social Vocabulary Pack. Jeremy Comfort. York Associates 1997.

Communication skills
Basic Telephone Training. Anne Watson-Delestrée. LTP 1992.
Better Business Writing. Alan Ram. York Associates Publications 1996.
Business Reports in English. Jeremy Comfort, Rod Revell and Chris Stott. CUP 1984.
Company to Company. Andrew Littlejohn. CUP 1994.
Effective Presentations. Jeremy Comfort. OUP 1994.
Effective Meetings. Jeremy Comfort. OUP 1995.
Effective Negotiating. Jeremy Comfort. OUP 1998.
Effective Socialising. Jeremy Comfort. OUP 1997.
Effective Telephoning. Jeremy Comfort. OUP 1996.
Exchanging Information. Mark Ellis and Nina O'Driscoll. Longman 1991.
Giving Presentations. Mark Ellis and Nina O'Driscoll. Longman 1992.
Handbook of Commercial Correspondence. A. Ashley. OUP 1992.
Language of Meetings. Malcolm Goodale. LTP 1988.
Making Contact. Nina O'Driscoll and Fiona Scott-Barrett. Longman 1991.
Meetings. Malcolm Goodale. LTP 1987.
Meetings and Discussions. Nina O'Driscoll and Adrian Pilbeam. Longman 1992.
Negotiating. Philip O'Connor, Adrian Pilbeam and Fiona Scott-Barrett. Longman 1992.
On the Line. K. Cripwell. OUP 1981.
Presenting in English. Mark Powell. LTP 1996.
Presenting Facts and Figures. David Kerridge. Longman 1992.
Social Contacts. Nick Brieger and Jeremy Comfort. Prentice Hall 1990.
Socialising. Mark Ellis and Nina O'Driscoll. Longman 1992.
Speaking Effectively. Jeremy Comfort et al. CUP 1994.
Take Another Letter. Geoffrey Myers. Phoenix ELT 1996.
Telephone Skills. David Hough. Heinemann 1993.
Telephoning. Longman 1992.
Telephoning in English. B. J. Naterop and R. Revell. CUP 1997.

Vocabulary
Build Your Business Vocabulary. John Flower. LTP 1990.
Business Terms. Hugh L'Estrange and Susan Norman. International Business Images 1995.

Business Words. D. Howard-Williams and C. Herd. Heinemann 1992.
Check Your Vocabulary for Business. David Riley. Peter Collin Publishing 1995.
Check Your Vocabulary for Computers. David Riley. Peter Collin Publishing 1995.
Check Your Vocabulary for Law. David Riley. Peter Collin Publishing 1996.
Check Your Vocabulary for Medicine. David Riley. Peter Collin Publishing 1995.
Key Terms in Personnel. Steve Flinders. York Associates 1995.
Key Words in Business. Bill Mascull. Collins Cobuild 1996.
Key Words in Science and Technology. Bill Mascull. Collins Cobuild 1997.
Key Words in the Media. Bill Mascull. Collins Cobuild 1995.
Test Your Business Vocabulary: Accountancy. Alison Pohl. Penguin English 1997.
Test Your Business Vocabulary: Elementary. Steve Flinders. Penguin English 1996.
Test Your Business Vocabulary: Finance. Simon Sweeney. Penguin English 1997.
Test Your Business Vocabulary: General. Joyce McKellen. Penguin English 1990.
Test Your Business Vocabulary: Hotel and Catering. Alison Pohl. Penguin English 1996.
Test Your Business Vocabulary: Intermediate. Steve Flinders. Penguin English 1997.
Test Your Business Vocabulary: Marketing. Simon Sweeney. Penguin English 1996.
Words at Work. David Horner and P. Strutt. CUP 1996.

Professional context

Accounting. Michael Sneyd. Prentice Hall 1994.
Advertising and the Promotion Industry. Maggie-Jo St John. Prentice Hall 1994.
At Your Service. Trish Stott and Angela Buckingham. OUP 1995.
English for Computing. Keith Boeckner and P. Charles Brown. OUP 1993.
English for International Banking and Finance. Jim Corbett. CUP 1990.
English for Law. Alison Riley. Macmillan 1991.
English for Telecoms. Ian Simpson and Derek Utley. York Associates 1995.
Finance. Nick Brieger and Jeremy Comfort. Prentice Hall BME 1992.
Financial English. Ian McKenzie. LTP 1996.
First Class. Trish Stott and Roger Holt. OUP
Insurance. Michael Sneyd. Prentice Hall 1996.
International Banking and Finance. Michael Sneyd. Prentice Hall 1992.
Marketing. Nick Brieger and Jeremy Comfort. Prentice Hall BME 1992.
Marketing. Maggie-Jo St John. Prentice Hall 1992.
Personnel. Nick Brieger and Jeremy Comfort. Prentice Hall BME 1992.
Production and Operations. Nick Brieger and Jeremy Comfort. Prentice Hall BME 1992.
Secretarial Contacts. Nick Brieger and Tony Cornish. Prentice Hall 1989.

Activities / case study / role play

Business Builder. P. Emmerson. Heinemann 1997.
Business Case Studies. R. Huggett. CUP 1994.
Business Communication Games. A. Lloyd and A. Preier. OUP 1996.
Business English Pair Work. Steve Flinders and Simon Sweeney. Penguin English 1996.
Business English Recipes. Judy Irigoin and Bonny Tsai. Longman 1995.
Business English Teacher's Resource Book. Sharon Nolan and Bill Reed. Longman 1992.
Business Games. Jenny Mawer. LTP 1992.
Decisionmaker. David Evans. CUP 1996.
International Business Role Plays. David Kerridge. Delta 1996.
More Business English Pair Work. Steve Flinders and Simon Sweeney. Penguin English 1998.

Reward Intermediate Business Resource Pack. David Riley. Heinemann 1996.
Reward Lower Intermediate Business Resource Pack. C.Benn and P.Dunnett. Heinemann 1995.

Reading
In Print. Rod Revell and Simon Sweeney. CUP 1992.

Dictionaries
Longman Concise Dictionary of Business English. J. H. Adam. Longman 1985.
Oxford Dictionary of Business English for Learners of English. Ed. A. Tuck. OUP 1993.
Plus any dictionary from the Peter Collins list (see Publishers.)

VIDEO
Business Assignments. Ken Casler and David Palmer. OUP 1989.
Communicating Styles. Derek Utley. York Associates 1995.
Effective Presentations. Jeremy Comfort and Derek Utley. OUP 1994.
Effective Meetings. Jeremy Comfort and Derek Utley. OUP 1995.
Effective Negotiating. Jeremy Comfort and Derek Utley. OUP 1998.
Effective Socialising. Jeremy Comfort and Derek Utley. OUP 1997.
Effective Telephoning. Jeremy Comfort and Derek Utley. OUP 1996.
Further Ahead. Andrew Bampfield. CUP.
Meeting Objectives. Vicki Hollett and Barnaby Newbolt. OUP.
Staying Ahead. Andrew Bampfield. CUP.

MULTIMEDIA AND PC
Business Challenges Interactive. Nina O'Driscoll and S. MacBurnie. Longman 1997.
Electronic Business Letter Writer. OUP 1997.
English for Business. University of Wolverhampton / Philips 1996/97.
M-Power Your Business English. Susan Norman and Hugh L'Estrange. IBI 1996.

ORGANISERS
Two systems designed to help you find your way around the bewildering array of materials on the market are:
The Complete Business English Course Generator (Mike Nelson. Media-Time) is a PC-based system for the design and implementation of BE courses which stores and provides cross-referenced information about many of the published materials on the market: available from the English Book Centre, Oxford (details below).
The BEBC Critical Directory of ELT Materials contains profiles of all the most popular ELT publications and has sections on Business English, video and computer materials: available from the Bournemouth English Book Centre (details below).

DISTRIBUTORS
Many thanks to Louis Garnade of the English Book Centre, Oxford for his help in the compilation of this list. All of the above titles are available from the EBC, 26 Grove Street, Oxford OX2 7JT, tel. 01865 514770, fax: 01865 513924, e-mail: 100622.2574@compuserve.com
Other major UK distributors are:
Bournemouth English Book Centre, 125 Charminster Road, Bournemouth, Dorset BH8 8UH, tel / fax: 01202 523103, e-mail: elt@bebc.co.uk
Cambridge International Book Centre, 42 Hills Road, Cambridge CB2 1LA, Tel: 01223 365400 Fax: 01223 312607

Keltic International, 39 Alexandra Road, Addlestone, Surrey KT15 2PQ, tel: 01932 820485, fax: 01932 849528, e-mail: janet@keltic.co.uk
The English Language Bookshop, 31 George Street, Brighton, Sussex BN2 1RH, tel: 01273 604864, fax: 01273 687280, e-mail: elb@pavilion.co.uk

Most of these also have their own very detailed catalogues.

For computer-based materials, the most comprehensive source is:
Wida Software, 2 Nicholas Gardens, London W5 5HY Tel: 0181 567 6941 Fax: 0181 840 6534
e-mail: widasoft@lang.wida.co.uk
compuServe 100014,2317

CHECKLIST 4

OTHER SOURCES OF MATERIAL FOR TEACHING BUSINESS ENGLISH

TEXT

A short list of ideas about how to build up banks of material fairly quickly. At York Associates, the resources centre contains books, magazines, realia, audio and video cassettes, computer software and material on CD ROM. The main categories for filing text-based materials are:
- language
- communication skills
- companies
- business area
- countries

The best regular sources of material are *The Financial Times*, *The Wall Street Journal* and the Business section of *The Economist* (weekly).
The Financial Times operates a free company annual report service and Barclays Bank publishes a free series of economic reports on a wide range of countries. Further information on all this is available in the (IATEFL) BESIG Resources Guide.

VIDEO

Management training videos are usually expensive since the companies which make them sell them to companies at corporate rates. In any case, get the catalogues of the big three producers:
Melrose Film Production Ltd., 16 Bromels Road, London SW4 OB4.
Video Arts Ltd., Dumbarton House, 68 Oxford Street, London W1N 0LH, tel: 0171 637 7288, fax: 0171 580 8103.
BBC for Business, 80 Wood Lane, London W12 0TT, tel: 0181 576 2361, fax: 0181 576 2867.

The Internet
The worlds of teaching, training and learning are being transformed by the Internet and change is so rapid that we shall not even attempt here to offer any but the most rudimentary guidance. Once again, membership of IATEFL and pertinent SIGs will help you to keep in touch with the explosion in relevant website addresses. The opportunity to download pages direct from the website of your students' company opens up all kinds of exciting possibilities. Here are some other Internet snippets:
A good introduction to EFL and the Internet at time of writing is "ELT Online: the rise of the Internet" in the July 1997 issue of the ELT Journal. David Eastment's definitive report on "The Internet and ELT" is available in web format at the British Council's website: www.britcoun.org/english
A list of Business English resources is available at www.infohaus./access/by-seller/Elite
IATEFL's own home page is at http://www.man.ac.uk/IATEFL/

Checklist 5
Business English Examinations

Centre	Examination
University of Cambridge Local Examinations Syndicate	Certificate in English for International Business and Trade Business English Certificates 1, 2 & 3
University of Oxford Delegacy of Oxford Exams	Oxford International Business English Certificate (OIBEC)
London Chamber of Commerce and Industry (LCCI)	English for Commerce English for Business (EFB) Spoken English for Industry and Tourism (SEFIC)
The Institute of Commercial Management (ICM)	ICM Certificate in Business English ICM Diploma in Business English

CEIBT
Candidates
From personal assistant up to middle management
Language Level
Around Cambridge Advanced (CAE)
Examination format and content
- Task-based to test communicative skills in English.
- Set in a multinational company
- Uses authentic material

- Role-playing to complete realistic tasks

Skills tested
- Reading and writing (2 hours). Tasks include writing a letter/fax/memo/report; checking a written text for mistakes; understanding the main points of authentic documents
- Listening (1 hour). Tasks include listening to a cassette containing authentic material (answerphone messages, office discussion) in order to take notes or compose a written text in reply.
- Oral transaction (15 minutes). A client of the company comes to meet you. In the interview you respond to his/her requests.

Time and place
May/June and November/December at approved centres in the UK and overseas (list available from UCLES)

Results
Grades are: Pass with distinction / Pass / Fail. Successful candidates receive a certificate.

UCLES has also developed a new suite of certified exams called Business English Certificates, available twice a year, at three levels (BEC1 - elementary / low intermediate, BEC2 - intermediate, BEC3 - advanced).
BEC1 is intended for those in lower to middle management, general office staff, staff in the tourist industry and students following business courses. BEC1 tests the use of English for carrying out business transactions, exchanging factual information, and establishing and maintaining business contacts. Successful candidates are expected to be able to understand or interpret the gist of a range of business texts including graphs, notices, correspondence and advertisements. Tasks include:
- form filling and letter writing
- extracting information from documents
- producing short reports and memos
- understanding recordings of announcements
- instructions and conversations
- discussing work, study and general topics.

BEC2 is aimed at candidates in management, staff in the tourist industry, senior clerical staff and students following business courses. BEC1 tests the use of English for negotiating business transactions, exchanging information, and establishing and maintaining business contacts. BEC2 contains a wider range of vocabulary and the tasks are more complex and demanding thanthose in BEC1. Successful candidates must show they understand the meaning of business texts, including advertisements, business correspondence, reports and articles. Tasks include:
- form filling and letter writing
- extracting information from documents

- producing reports and memos
- understanding meaning and tone of recordings of speeches, instructions and conversations
- discussing work, study and general topics.

BEC3 is intended for managers, particularly those dealing with English speakers, staff in the tourist industry, senior clerical staff, and students following business courses. BEC3 follows the same format as BEC1 and BEC2, testing the skills of reading and writing, listening and speaking but is more challenging in both content and structure. Candidates should be able to understand a variety of authentic business texts. Tasks include:
- form filling and letter writing
- understanding business documenets
- producing reports and memos
- understanding recordings of messages, instructions and conversations
- discussing work and study.

OIBEC
Candidates
For anyone with a practical knowledge of English. It is offered at two levels (First Level and Executive Level). In general it is appropriate for students:
- studying Business and Commerce
- aspiring to a career in international business
- who are already in business or managers who need to transfer their business/management skills into English

Language Level
First Level: ESU Framework Chart Levels 3 – 5. FCE
Executive Level: ESU Framework Chart Levels 6. CPE

Examination format and content
- Task-based to test communicative skills in English
- Authentic texts with simplified or staged tasks
- Two exam parts to each level
- First Level: 1 hour 55 minutes
- Executive Level: 2 hours 30 minutes

Skills tested
- Reading and writing (First Level 1 hour 15 minutes; Executive Level: 1 hour 35 minutes)
- Listening (First Level 20 minutes; Executive Level: 35 minutes)
- Speaking (Both Levels: 20 minutes)
- Three-days before the exam, candidates are sent a case-study booklet. This material forms the basis of the exam. Candidates are expected to apply the background knowledge they have gathered to perform practical tasks, including:
    - writing a business letter
    - making or assessing a job application

- correcting a memo
- listening to detailed information and responding
- making a flight reservation
- presenting an oral report
- discussing business objectives

Time and place
March, June and November at approved centres.
Results
Grades are:
Pass with score for communicative skills
Fail with profile of current performance
Successful candidates receive a certificate

EFC
Candidates
For anyone in the field of business or commerce.
Language Level
EFC is available at three levels:
First Level: ESU Framework Chart Levels 3; below FCE
Second Level: ESU Framework Chart Levels 6; around FCE
Third Level: ESU Framework Chart Levels 7; between FCE and CPE
Examination format and content
- Written exam based on language and content
- Tests basic knowledge of written language
- Credit given for appropriate use of complex sentences, punctuation, vocabulary and grammatical accuracy

Skills tested
First Level (2 hours)
- Three sections:
  - write 200 words on any one of 6 topics on general business matters
  - answer comprehension questions based on a text of 300 words
  - write a letter of about 100 words based on given data

Second Level (2- hours)
- Three sections:
  - write 300 words on any one of 6 topics on general business matters or current affairs
  - summarise a passage of about 400 words
  - write a letter of 150 – 200 words based on given data

Third Level (3 hours)
- Four sections:
  - write 400 – 500 words on any one of a number of topics requiring some knowledge of commercial practice and procedure
  - answer comprehension questions

- summarise a passage of about 500 words
- write a letter from an organisation to an individual concerning a specific transaction.

Time and place
First and Second Levels: March, May, June/ July and November/December
Third Level: May, June/ July and November/December

EFB
Candidates
For people working in offices in secretarial or personal assistant positions
Language Level
EFB is available at three levels:
First Level: ESU Framework Chart Levels 3/4; below FCE
Second Level: ESU Framework Chart Levels 5/6; around FCE
Third Level: ESU Framework Chart Level 7; between FCE and CPE
Examination format and content
- Written exam testing communication in business
- Tests basic knowledge of written language
- Credit given for appropriate use of complex sentences, punctuation, vocabulary, style, layout, maturity of expression and grammatical accuracy.

Skills tested
First Level (2 hours)
- Four tasks:
  - write a letter or memo within an organisation or between organisations
  - answer comprehension questions based on a text of 300 words
  - a look and think comprehension task based on graphic or numerical input
  - a look and write production task to label a diagram, flowchart or organisation chart, fill in a questionnaire, etc

Second Level (2- hours)
- Three tasks:
  - write a report, article or memo on a topic drawn from business or economic life
  - write a letter in reply to an incoming letter
  - rewrite a passage

Third Level (3 hours)
- Four tasks:
  - write a letter in reply to an incoming letter
  - write an internal report, based on raw data in the form of graphs, notes, charts, etc
  - comprehension of a passage to check understanding of factual content as well as argument, bias, etc

The York Associates Teaching Business English Handbook

– a conversation task involving the reformulation of a message
Time and place
First and Second Levels: March, May, June/ July and November/December
Third Level: May, June/ July and November/December

SEFIC
Candidates
A range of exams in practical skills at different levels.
Language Level
SEFIC is available at four levels:
Preliminary: ESU Framework Chart Level 3
Threshold: ESU Framework Chart Levels 4/5
Intermediate: ESU Framework Chart Level 6
Advanced: ESU Framework Chart Levels 7/8
Examination format and content
SEFIC is an oral exam
Skills tested

- *Preliminary (20 minutes: 5 per section)*

Four sections:
  – general conversation on candidate's personal history, work and interests
  – response to spoken instructions and relate to everyday objects
  – description of photographs
  – role play of everyday situation, eg booking in at a hotel, ordering a meal, etc

- *Threshold (25 – 35 minutes)*

Five sections:
  – introductory conversation on candidate's personal history, work and interests
  – description of actions in a sequence of photographs
  – comprehension of taped announcement
  – comprehension of written text – headline, ad, etc – or picture of everyday article – drinks machine, phone, etc – to check understanding of instructions
  – general conversation on candidate's personal history, work and interests

- *Intermediate (30 – 35 minutes)*

Four/five sections:
  – general conversation on candidate's personal history, work and interests
  – role play in official or information capacity
  – comprehension and summarisation of taped conversation
  – comprehension of business letter
  – special topic option to speak on a topic of candidate's own choice

- *Advanced (45 – 55 minutes)*
    Four sections:
    – general conversation on candidate's personal history, work and interests
    – presentation of candidate's work or special subject
    – comprehension and summarisation of taped conversation
    – comprehension and summarisation of English text – newspaper or magazine

Time and place
Available at any time of the year on any suitable premises worldwide.
Results
Distinction, Credit, Pass or Fail grades are awarded at each level.

ICM Certificate
Candidates
Business students, managers and executives + those who have completed higher level Business and Management Studies
Language Level
ESU Framework Chart Levels 5/6
Examination format and content
- Written exam + oral test

Skills tested
Written paper (5 tasks: 3 hours)
- Five tasks:
    – comprehension of factual business passage
    – write a letter in response to an incoming one
    – complete missing words from a passage
    – vocabulary test
    – summarise a passage of 150 words into 50 words
- *Oral test (10 minutes to read + 10 minutes to answer examiner's questions)*
    A short business case study on which questions are asked.

Time and place
12 times a year at an approved centre
Results
The following grades:
Certificate in Business English (Written) – if only written paper taken
Certificate in Business English (Written and Oral) – if both papers taken
Pass mark is 61%. Candidates scoring more than 85% are awarded the ICM Certificate in Business English with Distinction.

ICM Diploma
Candidates
Business students, managers and executives + those who have completed higher level Business and Management Studies

Language Level
ESU Framework Chart Levels 6/7
Examination format and content
Written exam + oral test
Skills tested
Written paper (5 tasks: 3 hours)
- Five tasks:
    - comprehension of newspaper article or business document
    - write a letter or memo based on instructions
    - complete missing words from a passage
    - vocabulary test
    - summarise a passage of 200 words into 100 words
- *Oral test (10 minutes to read + 10 minutes to answer examiner's questions)*
   A short business case study on which questions are asked.

Time and place
12 times a year at an approved centre
Results
The following grades:
Diploma in Business English (Written) – if only written paper taken
Diploma in Business English (Written and Oral) – if both papers taken
Pass mark is 61%. Candidates scoring more than 85% are awarded the ICM Diploma in Business English with Distinction.

ADDRESSES
University of Cambridge Local Examinations Syndicate (UCLES). 1 Hills Road, Cambridge, CB1 2EU, UK Tel: 01223 553311 Fax: 01223 460278

University of Oxford Delegacy of Local Exams. Ewert House, Summertown, Oxford, UK Tel: 01865 54291 Fax: 01865 510085

London Chamber of Commerce and Industry (LCCI) Examinations Board Marlowe House, Station Road, Sidcup, Kent, DA15 7BJ, UK
Tel: 0181 302 0261 Fax: 0181 302 4169

The Institute of Commercial Management (ICM), PO Box 125, Bournemouth, Dorset, BH1 1XF, UK Tel: 01202 290999 Fax: 01202 293497

CHECKLIST 6

LANGUAGE FOR EFFECTIVE COMMUNICATION

PRESENTATIONS

As a speaker moves through his/her presentation, it is vital to signal to the audience what he/she is going to do – to give a 'commentary' on recent and planned progress, so that the listeners know exactly where they are. The following list of link phrases is intended to start trainees thinking of the kind of language suitable for this 'commentary'. It is not complete, and will not be suitable for the personality of every speaker. Trainees should explore the range of phrases and, in the light of the subject of their talk, the style they prefer.

Introducing yourself and your presentation
Good morning / afternoon, …
… ladies and gentlemen.
My name is …
… and I am responsible for … here at …
I'd like to …
… say a few words to you today about …
… talk to you today about …
… explain to you today the main features of …
… describe the operation of …

Outlining the talk
I've divided my talk into five main parts.
The subject can be looked at under five main headings.
During my talk I'll be looking at five main areas.
First(ly) … second(ly) … third(ly) … fourth … fifth … finally
Ground rules
If you have any questions …
… please feel free to interrupt
… I'll be glad to try to answer them at end of my talk

Starting your first point
To start with …
First of all, then …
Firstly, …
Let me begin by saying …

Finishing a point
Well, that's all I have to say about …
So that, then, is …
That's all about …
Now we've dealt with …

Starting a new point
Now let's turn to my next point, which is ...
Let's move on now to ...
The next point I'd like to make is ...
Next we come to ...
Turning now to ...

Leaving the structure
Incidentally ...
By the way ...

Returning to your structure
Coming back to the subject of my talk ...
To come back to ...

Referring back
As I was saying earlier ...
As I mentioned earlier ...
If you remember, I said at the beginning ...

Referring forward
As we will see later, ...
Later, we'll be looking at ...
Later, I'd like to look at ...

Introducing your last point
And finally, ...
Lastly, ...
That brings me to my last point, which is ...

Summarising
So now, I'd just like to summarise the main points.
In brief, we have looked at ...
Let me sum up.

Concluding
In conclusion, ...
Well, that brings me to the end of my talk ...
That's all I have to say for now ...
Thank you for your attention.
Thank you for listening.

Inviting questions
And now, if you have any questions, I'll be glad to try to answer them.
Does anyone have any questions?
Are there any questions?
Any questions?
... Yes, your question, please.

Checklists

Checking that the questioner is satisfied
Does that answer your question?
I hope that answers your question.

Inviting further questions
Are there any more questions?
Any more questions?

Ending
If there are no more questions, I'd like to thank you for your attention.

MEETINGS

CONTROL PHRASES FOR THE CHAIRPERSON
Opening the meeting
Good morning / afternoon, everyone.
If we are all here, let's …
… get started
… start the meeting
… start

Welcoming and introducing participants
We're pleased to welcome …
It's a pleasure to welcome …
I'd like to introduce …
I don't think you've met …

Stating the purpose/objective/aim
We're here today to …
Our aim is to …
I've called this meeting in order to …
By the end of this meeting, we need a clear recommendation.

Giving apologies for absence
I'm afraid … can't be with us today. She is in …
I have received apologies for absence from … , who is in …

Reading the secretary's report of last meeting
First let's go over the report from the last meeting, which was held on …
Here are the minutes from our last meeting, which was on …

Dealing with Matters Arising
Peter, how is the IT project progressing?
Sarah, have you completed the report on the new accounting package?
Has everyone received a copy of Jeremy's report on his marketing visit?
So, if there are no other matters arising, let's move on to today's agenda.

Introducing the agenda
Have you all seen a copy of the agenda?

There are three items on the agenda – firstly, ... , secondly, ... and thirdly, ...
Shall we take the points in this order?
I suggest we take item 2 last.
Is there any other business?

Allocating roles (secretary, participants and chairperson)
... has agreed to take the minutes.
... , would you mind taking the minutes?
... has kindly agreed to give us a report on this matter.
... will lead point 1, ... point 2, and ... point 3.

Agreeing the ground rules for the meeting (contributions, timing, decision-making, etc)
We will hear a short report on each point first, followed by a discussion round the table.
I suggest we go round the table first.
The meeting is due to finish at ...
We'll have to keep each item to ten minutes. Otherwise we'll never get through.
We may need to vote on item 5, if we can't get a unanimous decision.

Introducing the first item
So, let's start with ...
Shall we start with ... ?
So, the first item on the agenda is ...
Pete, would you like to kick off?
Martin, would you like to introduce this item?

Closing an item
I think that covers the first item.
Shall we leave that item?
If nobody has anything else to add, ...
Next item
 ... let's move onto the next item
The next item on the agenda is ...
Now we come to the question of ...

Asking for contributions
We haven't heard from you yet, George. What do you think about this proposal?
Would you like to ad anything, Anne?
Anything to add, Helen?

Handing over to another person
I'd like to hand over to Mark, who is going to lead the next point.
Right, Dorothy, over to you.

Keeping the meeting on target (time, relevance, decisions)
We're running short of time.
Please be brief.
I'm afraid we've run out of time.
We'll have to leave that to another time.
I'm afraid that's outside the scope of this meeting.
We're beginning to lose sight of the main point.
Keep to the point, please.
I think we'd better leave that for another meeting.

Checklists

Are we ready to make a decision?
Shall we vote on Mary's proposal?

Clarifying
Let me spell out ...
Is that clear?
Do you all see what I'm getting at?
to clarify
to explain
to interpret
to put another way
to put in other words
to recap

Summarising
Before we close, let me just summarise the main points.
To sum up, ...
In brief, ...
Shall I go over the main points?

a summary
a report
a write-up

Agenda completed
Right, it looks as though we've covered the main items.
Is there any other business?

Agreeing time, date and place for next meeting
Can we fix the next meeting, please?
So, the next meeting will be on ... (day), the ... date) of ... (month) at ... (time) in the meeting room. Is that okay for everyone?
What about the following Wednesday? How is that?
So, see you all then.

Thanking participants for attending
I'd like to thank Marianne and Jeremy for coming over from London.
Thank you all for attending.
Thanks for your participation.

Closing meeting
The meeting is closed.
I declare the meeting closed.

CONTROL PHRASES FOR THE PARTICIPANTS

Getting the chairperson's attention
(Mister/madam) chairman.
Excuse me for interrupting.
May I come in here?

Giving and seeking opinions
I'm sure/convinced/positive that ...
I (really) feel that ...
In my opinion ...
I tend to think that ...
Are you sure/convinced/positive that ...
Do you (really) think that ... ?
Am I right in thinking that ...

Commenting
That's interesting ...
Good point!
I see what you mean.

Agreeing and disagreeing
I totally agree with you.
Up to a point I agree with you, but ...
(I'm afraid) I can't agree

Advising and suggesting
Let's ...
We should ...
Why don't you ...
How about ...
I suggest/recommend that ...

Requesting information and action
Please, could you ...
I'd like you to ...
I wonder if you could ...

Dealing with communication problems
Asking for repetition
I didn't catch that. Could you repeat that, please?
Sorry, I missed that. Could you say it again, please?

Asking for clarification
I don't quite follow you. What exactly do you mean?
I don't see what you mean. Could we have some more details, please?

Asking for verification
You did say March, didn't you? ('did' is stressed)
Is it true that we'll be moving in March?

Asking for spelling
Could you spell that, please?

Correcting information
Sorry, I think you misunderstood what I said. The move will be in March.
Sorry, that's not quite right. We'll be here until March.

PHRASES FOR THE SECRETARY

Listing the names of the participants
Present: ... (names or initials)
Apologies for absence received from: ... (names or initials)

Describing the topics discussed
... (name) reported on/presented/considered/discussed/evaluated/proposed ...

Giving details of arguments for and against
... (name) pointed out/observed/stated that ...
... (name) disagreed with/voiced reservations about/opposed/objected to ...

Describing the decisions made
The meeting agreed to ...
It was (unanimously) agreed that we would ...
... (item) was postponed until the next meeting on ...

Describing voting details
Three voted for the motion; two voted again.
The motion was carried by three votes to two.
The proposal was defeated by three votes

to two.

Describing follow-up actions to be carried out (who, what and when)
... (name) will prepare a report by ... date)
... (name) agreed to evaluate the new software by ... (date)
It was agreed that ... (name) would present the findings to the next meeting on ... (date)

Showing the date, time and place of the next meeting
The next meeting will be held on ... (date) at ... (time) in ... (place)
Next meeting ... (time) on ... (date) in ... (place)

Telephoning

The following list of phrases trace a call through from beginning to end and correspond to the building blocks shown in chapter 4. They follow two patterns – firstly when making a call and secondly when receiving a call.
Making a Call
Identifying yourself
My name is ... (first introduction)
This is ... here.
... speaking.
Asking to speak to someone
Could I speak to ... please?
Could you put me through to ... please?
Can I have extension 351 please?
Could I speak to someone who deals with ... ?
You might hear: (see Receiving a call)
Who's calling?
Could you tell me what it's about?
Giving more information
It's in connection with ...
It's about ...
Giving the reason for the call
I'm calling about ...
I'm phoning to tell you ...
The reason I'm calling is ...

Showing you understand
I see
I understand
Right / Fine / Okay

Leaving a message
Could you give him a message?
Could you ask her to call me back?
Could you tell her I'll call back later?

Communication problems
Could you repeat that?
I'm sorry, I didn't catch your name.
Could you speak a little slower?
...
louder?
It's a very bad line. I'll call you back.
Getting the information right
Could you spell that please?
Could you go over that again please?
Let me just repeat that ...

Pre-closing
Summarise main points
So, let me just go over the main points.
Let me just repeat what you said.
So, if I understand you correctly, the situation is ...

Thanking
Thanks very much for your help.
I'm grateful for your assistance.
Thanks a lot.

Responding to thanks
Not at all.
You're welcome.
Don't mention it.
Confirming the arrangement
I look forward to ...
... seeing you on ... (date) at ... (time)
... hearing from you soon.
... meeting you in ... (place)

Polite fomulae
Nice speaking to you.

You might hear:
Nice speaking to you, too.

Closing the call
See you soon
Speak to you soon
Goodbye
Bye
Receiving a Call
Identifying yourself
Harry Jones
Harry Jones speaking

You might hear: (see Making a call)
Could I speak to Harry Jones?
You can reply:
Speaking.

Helping the caller
Can I help you?
Who would you like to speak to?

Asking for identification
Who's calling, please?
And who's speaking, please?

Asking for further information
What's it in connection with?
What's it about, please?

Making excuses
I'm afraid ... is not available at the moment

I'm afraid ...   is out
                     is in a meeting
                     is with a customer at
the moment
I'm sorry but ...   is on holiday
                     is not in the office
                     is on the other line at
present.
I'm afraid his line's engaged.
Do you want to hold?

Taking a message
Would you like to leave a message?
May I take a message?
Can I take your name and number?
Can I get him to call you back?

Pre-closing
See 'Making a call'

Polite formulae
Thanks for calling.

You might hear:
Not at all. It's been nice speaking to you.
You're welcome

Closing the call
Goodbye
Bye.

NEGOTIATION

The processes
to negotiate
to strike a bargain
to bargain
to reach agreement
to discuss
to draft a contract
to persuade
to sign the contract
to compromise
to implement the agreement
to make a deal
to break the contract

The subject of negotiation
price
warranties and guarantees
delivery and terms
insurance
discount
quality control
payment and credit
penalties
exclusivity
legal jurisdiction
licences

Checklists

Creating the right environment
Language for:
- introducing yourself
- making small talk

Defining the issues
Stating the agenda
OK. Shall we start?
Our position is as follows:
We would like to buy ...
We are interested in selling ...
We need to reach agreement about ...
We are keen to make a decision about ...
The aim/purpose/target/objective of this negotiation is to solve the problem over ...
Clarifying the agenda
So, if we understand you correctly, you want to sell ...
So, are we right in thinking that you would like us to sell ... ?
We fully understand your views/position ...
... But what exactly do you want us to do?
... But what would you actually like us to do?
... But what precisely are you offering?
So, then, can you just confirm that your position is ... ?

Establishing opening positions
Price
In your proposal
    your asking price is ...
    you have set the price at ....
    you have fixed the cost at ...
price   fee
cost   payment
charge   tax
We are willing to pay ...
Our initial offer is ...

Delivery and terms
In addition,   we/you can deliver the goods on 25th July.
                        we can supply the products by 25th July.
                        you can arrange delivery to our warehouse from stock.
                        you can organise shipment by truck to our site.
Our position is that
    we need the goods by 20th July.
    the goods must be with us by 20th July.
Can you arrange delivery to our site by truck?

site
office
plant
premises
warehouse
shop
store
supermarket
factory
workshop
by post   by ferry
by special postal delivery by train
by truck   by plane
by van   by airfreight
by boat

However,
    you expect us to provide transport and insurance.
However,
    you are not prepared to cover transport.
    you do not agree to pay for ...

on Monday (days of the week)
on 25th July (dates)
by 25th July (deadlines)
in July (months)
next week/month
in 2 months

Payment and credit
We expect payment by bank transfer within 90 days.
    90 days after invoice.
    90 days after order.
Our normal payment terms are by letter of credit.
Do you accept our payment terms?
We do not accept the payment terms?
We do not normally pay ...
    in cash

by cheque
by bank transfer
by letter of credit

Discount
However,
    we can offer an initial discount of 5%.
    we can discount the initial order by 5%.
But we are prepared to reduce the total price by 5%.
What discount can you offer?

Exclusivity
Can you offer us exclusivity?
We are looking for an exclusive agent.
We need an exclusive distributor.
We are not prepared to   act as an exclusive representative.
    offer exclusivity.
agent
distributor
representative

Licences
What licence can you offer?
We are prepared to offer a licence to sell the product.
We cannot grant a licence to manufacture the product.
The licence will initially be limited to 5 years.

Warranties and guarantees
What warranties and guarantees do you offer?
We warrant the goods for a period of 5 years.
We guarantee the products against normal defects for 3 years?
We cover all parts and labour for 1 year.
In that case,
    we will replace the goods.
    repair the equipment free of charge.
We will cover all labour costs.
We will fix the problem on site.
You must return the goods to base.
We cannot guarantee the goods against ...
    breakdown
    normal wear and tear

Insurance
Will you insure the goods during transit?
We will insure the goods during transportation.
We will cover the equipment CIF.
CIF
    cost, insurance and freight
FOB
    free on board

Quality control
What quality control measures do you take?
All goods are tested before they leave the factory.
The products are fully checked for defects.
We follow a TQC programme.
We have ISO 9000.

Penalties
What happens if anything goes wrong?
What compensation will you pay if ... ?
We will claim compensation if ...
    ... you don't deliver on time.
    ... the goods are delayed.
    ... the equipment breaks down.

Legal jurisdiction
What happens if there is a dispute?
Any disputes will be settled according to French law.
We resolve any disagreements by arbitration.

dispute	breach of contract
disagreement	conflict
law	mediation
court of law	
international court of justice	
arbitration	

HANDLING THE OFFER AND COUNTER-OFFER

Positive
That's great.
(That's a) good/excellent/great idea.
We accept/agree.
We can accept your payment

Checklists

terms/delivery terms/discount terms
We agree to follow the quality control procedures.
We are in agreement over penalty clauses.

Partial
Yes, but ...
We're on the right track.
We're getting there.

Negative
That's unacceptable.
That's out of the question.
We can't accept that.
We don't agree to that.
We cannot accept your warranty terms/insurance terms
We don't agree to follow the legal procedures.
We are not in agreement over compensation clauses.

Testing the other side's case
Have you given us all the relevant facts?
On what are those figures based?
We have heard that your normal prices are ...
    normal delivery terms are ...
    normal discount terms are ...
    normal warranty terms are ...
Could you explain how you reach ...
We don't follow the logic of your argument.
If your normal prices are ... ,
    then we expect ...
Could you explain how you got to those figures?

Strengthening your case
If we accept your prices, then we will
    have to raise our prices.
    your delivery terms, then we will have to delay production.
    your payment terms, that will increase our costs.
That will not be good for our business.
If you can reduce your price by ... , then we will ...
If you are prepared to speed up delivery by ... , then we will ...
If you are willing to reconsider your payment terms, then we will ...

... look at prices for our next contract.
... review delivery for the next consignment.
... discuss payment with our bank for the next order.

Handling stalemate
We are very far apart on this issue.
Our positions are very different on the question of ...
I don't think we can resolve this matter now.
Let's see where we agree ...
Shall we summarise the points of agreement ...
    ... and then take a short break.
    ... and then adjourn till this afternoon.
So far, we've agreed on the following points: ...
We disagree on ...
So we'll come back to those issues after the break.

Clinching the deal
We have covered a lot of ground in this meeting.
We cannot change our offer.
This is our final offer.
We have reached agreement on ...
You have accepted our terms on ...
We have not reached agreement on ...
You cannot accept our terms on ...
Let me go over all the details again.
Have I covered everything?
Do you agree?
Do you accept these terms?

Getting it in writing
I will draft an outline agreement.
Can you prepare a draft contract?
I will send the agreement to you for your comments.
Please send the draft contract to me for our comments.
After the contract/agreement has been signed, ...
    ... we can   make the goods.
                   deliver the equipment.

The legal aspects
contract

indemnity
parties to the contract
to sign a contract
signatories to the contract
scope of the contract
terms of the contract
clauses of the contract
payment
delivery
insurance

force majeure
to break a contract
breach of contract
disputes
damages
compensation
arbitration
annex
appendix

CHECKLIST 7

AREAS OF SPECIALIST VOCABULARY

GENERAL MANAGEMENT

achievement
administration
advertising
analysis
apprentice
arbitration
assets
audit
authority
automation
background
bargaining
behaviour
board of directors
break-even
budget
capacity
capital
career
cash
cashflow
challenge
channel of
    communication
change
charity
client
coaching
colleague
commission

commitment
committee
communication
compensation
competence
competition
computer
conflict
confrontation
consensus
consumer
control
co-operation
co-ordination
corporate
cost
culture
customer
debt
decentralisation
decision
delegation
department
dependence
development
discipline
discrimination
distribution
diversification
division

downsizing
duty
economy
effectiveness
efficiency
employee
employer
employment
environment
equipment
ethics
expectation
expenses
expert
failure
feedback
finance
fixed assets
fixed costs
flexitime
forecasting
franchising
goal
group
growth
hierarchy
human resources
incentive
income
influence

information
innovation
input
institution
integration
international
inventory
job
    description
    design
    experience
    rotation
    satisfaction
title
knowledge
labour
leadership
liabilities
line manager
loyalty
management
market
media
middle manager
motivation
multinational
needs
negotiation
network
objectives

Checklists

off-the-job	premises	resource	storage
on-the-job	pricing	responsibility	strategy
operations	priority	reward	stress
management	problem solving	risk	subordinate
organisation	process	role	supply
chart	product	rule	supplier
organisational	production	safety	task
change	productivity	scheduling	team
culture	profit	security	technology
structure	project	selection	theory
output	management	service	top manager
performance	team	share	training
appraisal	quality	shareholder	transportation
personality	questionnaire	skill	unit
personnel	recruitment	source	value
planning	redundancy	sponsorship	work design
plant	remuneration	staff	working
policy	research and	stakeholder	conditions
power	development	standard	

ADMINISTRATION

Administrative staff	archive(s)	hole punch	**Communication**
administrator	file (n)	keyboard	compliments slip
clerk	file (v)	paper clip	letterhead
office manager	sort	PC	post/mail
assistant	**Equipment**	printer	correspondence
personal assistant	answerphone	photocopier	send a fax
secretary	computer	stapler	an e-mail
typist	filing cabinet	telephone	a letter
Information	fax machine	typewriter	
organisation	hanging files		

CUSTOMER SERVICE

General	export	run out of	barter
agent	fetch	scarce	conditions of sale
busy	file	schedule (n)	haggle
buy	customer file	schedule (v)	negotiate
cater for	handle	service	negotiable
custom	import	after-sales	negotiation
customer	install	service industry	**Complaints**
customize	item	tariff	blame
deal	label	trade	claim
delay	off-peak	trade in	compensate
demand	off-season	triplicate	damage
discontinue	paperwork	in triplicate	damages
duty	part-exchange	**Negotiating**	fault
exchange	delivery	bargain (n)	guarantee
exempt	quality	bargain (v)	hazard

insure
   insurance claim
   insurance cover
   insurance policy
   insurance premium
overdue
repair
spoil
Payment
credit
   credit note
hire purchase
invoice (n)
invoice (v)
lease (n)
lease (v)
outright purchase
over-charged
overpaid
pay
   pay in advance
   pay by cheque
   pay in cash
   payable
   payment
prepaid
rebate
settle
statement
Orders
acknowledge
acknowledgement
available
   availability
bring forward
bulk
   in bulk
cancel
   cancellation
confirm
notify
offer
order
   fulfill an order
   on order
   back order
quote
   quotation
place an order
postpone
ready
receive
receipt
reorder
repeat order
shortage
stock
   in stock
   out of stock

DISTRIBUTION

Transport
cargo
carriage
cif
crate
deliver
   delivery
   delivery note
   delivery time
depot
dispatch
distribute
duty
enclose
envelope
f.o.b.
forward
freight
haul
in transit
lading
   bill of lading
load
mail (n)
mail (v)
pack
package
pallet
ship
   shipment
tanker
unload
Channels
branch
bottleneck
cash and carry
chain
channel
consignment
dealer
department store
direct export
franchise
middleman
network
quota
retail
   retail outlet
   retailer
scarce
sourcing
storage
tariff
warehouse
wholesale

FINANCE

General
accounts
   accountancy
   accountant
acquire
   acquisition
allocate
back
   backing
backdate
bankrupt
   to go bankrupt
   bankruptcy
bid
black
   in the black
books
   keep the books
   bookkeeper
borrow
break even
budget
capital
cash
cheque (US: check)
   bounce a cheque
cost
fixed costs
running costs
variable costs
credit
currency
debt
   debtor
deduct
defer
due
earn
   earnings
finance
funds
income
insider dealing
insolvent
interest
   interest rate
lend
   lender
liquid
   liquidity
loan
overdraw
   overdraft
owe
petty cash

Checklists

profit
   profitable
   profitability
raise
rate
recover
red
   in the red
save
   savings
subsidise
   subsidy
treasurer
   treasury
Investment
base rate
blue chips
bond
broker
dealer
debenture
dividend
earnings per share
equity
   equities
gross yield
invest
   investment
portfolio
   portfolio

management
preference shares
premium
securities
share (US: stock)
   shareholder
   (US: stockholder)
Financial statements
asset
   current assets
   fixed assets
   intangible assets
audit
   auditor
balance sheet
cash flow
   negative cash
   flow
debit
depreciate
   depreciation
expenditure
   expenses
gearing
goodwill
gross
   gross margin
   gross profit
half-year
   half-yearly

results
inventory
ledger
   sales/purchase
   ledger
liabilities
   current
   liabilities
margin
overhead
   overheads (n)
profit and loss
   account (US:
   income
   statement)
quarterly
reserves
results
retained earnings
return
   return on
   investment
turnover
working capital
write off
Payment
bad debt
bank charges
bank draft
bank statement

blank cheque
convert
credit
   credit limit
   credit rating
direct debit
letter of credit
demand
discount
   factoring
invoice
outstanding
Tax
capital gains tax
corporation tax
declare
   tax declaration
fiscal
income tax
tax allowance
tax avoidance
tax deductible
tax evasion
tax loophole
tax relief
tax threshold
value added tax

LEGAL

General
abide by
abolish
abuse (n)
abuse (v)
accuse
appeal
arbitrate
   arbitration
bail
bequest
bond
case
   case law
civil law
claim (n)
claim (v)
   claimant

conflict
   conflict of
   interest
copyright
court
   go to court
   take someone
   to court
damages
endow
   endowment
fee
illegal
indemnify
   indemnity
irrevocable
   irrevocable
   letter of credit

judicial
jurisdiction
law
   within the law
   outside the law
   against the law
legal
liability
   limited liability
litigant
loophole
   tax loophole
oath
offence
   offend
ombudsman
party
   third party

patent
   file a patent
   application
penalty
   penalty clause
plea
plead
pledge
precedent
quorum
   quorate
sue
suit
trademark
tribunal
unjust
unlawful
waive

The York Associates Teaching Business English Handbook

Property
access
estate
hereditary
mortgage
premises
tenure
vacant
    vacant
    possession
People
actuary
advocate
attorney
bailiff
barrister
judge
jury
lawyer
legal advisor
notary
paralegal

solicitor
Contracts
agreement
clause
settlement
settle
    settle out of
    court
Crimes
blackmail
break the law
bribe
    bribery
embezzle
    embezzlement
extort
    extortion
fraud
    fraudulent
kickback
misconduct
    professional

misconduct
swindle
Types of company
associate company
consortium
corporate
    corporation
firm
holding company
limited company
listed company
parent company
private limited
    company (Ltd.)
public limited
    company (PLC)
subsidiary
Financial problems
bankrupt
    bankruptcy
debt
foreclose

foreclosure
insolvent
    insolvency
liquidate
    liquidation
    liquidator
receiver
    receivership
Employee relations
conciliation
grievance
industrial tribunal
labour law
strike
Legal problems
breach of contract
infringe copyright
    infringement
injunction

MARKETING

General
capture
cartel
compete
    competition
    competitor
    competitive
competitive pricing
domestic market
down-market
exhibit
    exhibition
flop
forecast
goodwill
logo
market
    down-market
    market leader
    market niche
    market
    penetration
    market
    segmentation
    market share
    market survey

up-market
mass-market
outlet
saturate
sector
segment
target
territory
Customers
end-user
client
Products
brand
    brand leader
    brand loyalty
cannibalism
commodity
diversify
feature
flagship
generic
giveaway
goods
    industrial goods
label
launch

life cycle
portfolio
positioning
prototype
range
sell-by date
shelf-life
tailor-made
trade mark
white goods
Advertising
account executive
advertise
    advertisement
art director
artwork
audience
banner
brief
broadsheet
brochure
canvass
caption
catalogue
circular
copy

endorse
    endorsement
flier
jingle
layout
magazine
media
    mass media
    media coverage
pamphlet
periodical
    scientific
    periodical
poster
prospectus
publication
ratings
readership
slogan
spot
tabloid
testimonial
viewer
Pricing
bargain
ceiling

Checklists

price ceiling
creaming
cut-price
discount
elastic
going rate
gross margin
index
inelastic
introductory offer
knockdown
margin
mark up
MRP = (Manufacturer's Recommended Price)
overheads
premium
rate
refund
retail
    retailer
retail price
    skimming
surcharge
value
wholesale
    wholesaler
    wholesale price
Public Relations
identity
    corporate identity
image
    corporate image
lobby
press
    press officer
    press relations
    press release
sponsor
    sponsorship

HUMAN RESOURCES

General
absent
    absenteeism
alcoholism
ambition
    ambitious
aptitude
canteen
career
conditions
    working conditions
    conditions of employment
core time
employ
    employee
    employer
    employment
equal opportunity
flexitime
head
hire
human resources
job
    job centre
    job satisfaction
labour
    labour relations
lead
    leader
    leadership
liaison
loyal
    loyalty
manpower
plant
position
profession
punctuality
shift
    shift work
shop
    shopfloor
    shop steward
sick
    sick note
trade union
vacation
working hours
Types of jobs
blue-collar
board of directors
clerk
management
    junior/middle/ senior management
manager
    line manager
    staff manager
manual
    manual worker
skilled
    semi-skilled
    unskilled
shift worker
staff
subordinate
superior
white-collar
Disputes
go-slow
grievance
industrial
    industrial action
    industrial relations
    industrial unrest
militant
picket
strike
work to rule
Recruitment
applicant
    application form (US: application blank)
apply
appoint
candidate
c.v. (curriculum vitae)
experience
fill (a position)
induction
interview
    interviewee
    interviewer
job description
qualifications
    qualified
    well-qualified
    unqualified
recruit
    recruitment
reference
select
    selection board
shortlist
track record
vacancy
Leaving
dismiss
    dismissal
fire
hand in one's notice
lay off
notice
redundant
    redundancy
resign
    resignation
retire
    retirement
    early retirement
sack
turnover
Assessment
appraise
    appraisal
competence
grade
perform
    performance appraisal
probation
talent
vocation
Training & Development
apprentice
    apprenticeship
coach
course
facilitate
mentor

promote workshop compensate pay package
progress **Remuneration** deduction payroll
protégé bargain incentive pension
seminar   collective income perk
train bargaining merit profit-sharing
   training benefit   merit pay reward
   on-the-job   fringe benefit overtime salary
   training   sickness benefit pay wage

PRODUCTION AND OPERATIONS

Production place efficiency make-to-stock materials
factory   efficient output   handling
plant goods productive raw materials
site   finished goods   productivity **Stock**
unit intermittent prototype stock
workshop production schedule   stock levels
Quality line set-up time   in stock
accurate   assembly line slack   out of stock
   accuracy   assembly line throughput   stock control
assess   manager work-in progress   stockpile
defect   line worker **Resources** store
evaluate man bill of materials   storage
inspect   manning equip **Maintenance**
quality off-the-shelf   equipment break down
   quality produce facility failure
   assurance   production   facilities fault
   quality circle **Planning** fixtures   faulty
   quality control backlog inventory maintain
reject batch   raw materials   maintenance
   reject rate   batch size   inventory repair
scrap capacity   work-in- reliable
zero defect critical path analysis   progress   reliability
Process cycle time   inventory shut down
assemble delivery cycle machine **Work organisation**
   assembly downtime   machinery job evaluation
   assembly line flow MRP =   job rotation
automate   flow rate (Materials   job sharing
   automation idle Requirements overtime
component job lot Planning) shift
continuous process lead time just-in-time   night shift
convert make-to-order materials workload

PURCHASING

General supplier management
auction **People** vendor   inventory
buy buyer **Functions**   control
supply   junior buyer inventory logistics
   supplies   senior buyer   inventory materials
   purchaser

Checklists

management
vendor appraisal
Finance
bill
   billing
currency
   weak currency
   strong currency
Supply & Demand
buyer
buyers' market
sellers' market
demand
   under-demand
   over-demand
supply
   under-supply
   over-supply
Tendering process
accept
reject
tender
   call for tenders
   closed tender
   open tender
   submit a tender/an offer
   tender evaluation
   tender specifications
Documents
letter of intent
purchase order
Price negotiation
bottom-line
cut
margin
target price

RESEARCH & DEVELOPMENT (R&D)

General
analyze
   analysis
   analytical
breakthrough
carry out
develop
   commercial development
feasible
   feasibility
innovate
   innovation
laboratory (lab)
me-too product
patent
   file/register a patent
pipeline
   in the pipeline
search
study (n)
study (v)
survey (n)
survey (v)
tailor
   tailor-made
test (n)
test (v)
trial (n)
trial (v)
Research
academic research
applied research
pure research
Research people
analyst
research assistant
scientist
technician
   lab technician

SALES

General
gift
give-away
sales call
   conference
   message
   target
sample
Selling People
field sales
inside salesperson
sales assistant
   manager
salesforce
salesman
saleswoman
salesperson
Buying people
client
customer
opinion leader
prospect
Types of selling
door-to-door sales
direct sales
hard selling
personal selling
soft selling
telephone sales
Sales organisation
sales area
   region
   territory
territory management

Abbreviations

Teaching

AmE	American English
BE	Business English
BESIG	Business English Special Interest Group (of IATEFL)
BrE	British English
CBT	Computer-Based Training
CEIBT	Certificate in English for Business and Trade (UCLES exam)
CertTEB	Certificate in Teaching English for Business
CPE	Certificate of Proficiency in English
CUP	Cambridge University Press
EFB	English for Business (LCCI exam)
EFC	English for Commerce (LCCI exam)
ELT	English Language Teaching
ESP	English for Specific Purposes
ESU	English Speaking Union
FCE	First Certificate in English
IATEFL	International Association of Teachers of English as a Foreign Language
ICM	Institute of Commercial Management
LCCI	London Chamber of Commerce and Industry
OIBEC	Oxford International Business English Certificate
OUP	Oxford University Press
PC	Personal Computer
SEFIC	Spoken English for Industry and Tourism
TEFL	Teaching English as a Foreign Language
TESOL	Teachers of English to Speakers of Other Languages
UCLES	University of Cambridge Local Examinations Syndicate

Business

CEO	Chief Executive Officer
MD	Managing Director

References

References in the Text

Drucker P. (1967). *The Effective Executive*, Heinemann.
Follett M. P. (1918) *The New State*. Gloucester, Mass.: Peter Smith.
Honey P. and H. Mumford (1992 new edition). *A Manual of Learning Styles*.
Kotler P. (1980). *Marketing Management*. Maidenhead: P. Honey.
Mole J. (1995). *Mind Your Manners: Managing Business Cultures in Europe*. London: Nicholas Brealey Publishing.

Mecson M. H., M. Albert and F. Khedouri (1985). *Management: Individual and Organisational Effectiveness*. 2nd Ed. New York: Harper and Row.
Stoner, Freedman and Gilbert (1991). *Management* 6th Ed. New Jersey: Prentice Hall Inc.

Information about the leadership study carried out by Unabridged Communications (Chapter 5) is available from Unabridged Communications, 2728 North Washington Boulevard, Alexandria, Virginia, 22302 USA.

OTHER USEFUL REFERENCES

Business Management
Hunningher E. (ed.) (1986). *The Manager's Handbook*. London: Sphere.
Kempner T. (ed.) (1987). *The Penguin Management Handbook*. London: Penguin.
Lawrence P. and Elliott K. (1985). *Introducing Management*. London: Penguin.
Pitfield R. (1980). *Administration in Business*. W.H.Allen & Co.
Walsh J. (1986). *The Manager's Problem Solver*. London: Sphere.

Training
Brendan and Wheelan (ed.) (1987). *Training Theory and Practice*. NTL Institute for Applied Behavioural Science.
Goad T. (1982). *Delivering Effective Training*. University Associates Inc.

INDEX

Academic institutions, 11
Accuracy, 4, 39-42, 63, 110-111, 114-115
Activist learning style, 108
Activity, case study and role play books, 158
Administration, 29
Administration Department, 27
Administration vocabulary, 181
Agenda for a simulated meeting, 53
Assessing entry levels, 99
Associated company, 19
Audio materials, 130

Behavioural approaches to leadership, 69
Behavioural movements in management theory, 22
Behavioural Scientists, 23
Book and software distributors, 159-160
Brainstorming meetings, 48
Briefing meetings, 48
Budget allocation negotiations, 62
Building high performance teams, 74-75
Business English Certificates, 162
Business English learners, 15
Business English methodology, 15

Business English programmes, 15
Business English trainers, 15
Business English versus General English, 15
Business sectors, 33
Buyer-seller negotiations, 62

Case studies as evaluation tools, 95
Certificate in English for International Business and Trade, 161-162
Chief Executive Officer, 26, 27
Classical organisation theory, 21
Classroom as bridge, 122-124

Closed group courses, 89
Closed-scale evaluation, led by reviewer, 140
Closed-scale evaluation, written feedback, 140
Coach training style, 126
Coherence and cohesion in writing, 66
Committee meetings, 48
Communication networks, 94
Communication skills books, 157
Communication skills, 5, 6, 8, 12, 35, 88
Communicative competence scale, 100
Company culture, 82-83
Company hierarchy, 24-25
Company meetings, 48
Company organigram, 26
Competence, 104-105
Computer systems, 30
Conciseness in writing, 65-66
Content in writing, 65
Content of a presentation, 44
Context-based models of leadership, 69
Control phrases for chairpersons, 171-173
Control phrases for participants in meetings, 174
Controlling, 28
Course evaluation forms, 141, 143
Course evaluation, 139
Course inputs and outputs, 102
Course objectives, 5, 87-99
Course registration, 89
Coursebooks, 156
Cultural awareness, 7
Culture onion, 81
Current developments in leadership, 70
Customer service, 28
Customer Service Department, 27

Customer service vocabulary, 181

Decision-making meetings, 48
Delegation, 75-79
Delegation and communication, 78-79
Delegation in practice, 77
Delegation to non-humans, 77
Delivery of a presentation, 44
Developing effectiveness, 137
Developing fluency, 137
Dictionaries, 159
Director training style, 126
Discourse patterns, 36
Distribution, 29
Distribution Department, 27
Distribution vocabulary, 181
Division of labour, 24
Drafting the course report, 144

Early models of leadership, 69
Effectiveness, 4, 39, 41-43, 63-64, 110-111,114-115, 138
Employer-employee negotiations, 62
Ending the course, 132-138
English for Business examinations, 165-166
English for Commerce examinations, 164-165
Equipment, 130-131
ESP family, 8
Evaluation, 110-111
Evolution of management, 19-20

Factors in delegation, 76
Fayol, Henri, 21-22
Features of materials, 128-129
Feedback loop, 104-105
Feedback questions, 140
Finance, 29

Finance Department, 27
Finance vocabulary, 182
Financial accounting, 29-30
Fluency, 4, 39-42, 63-64, 110-111,114-115, 138
Follett, Mary Parker, 20
Freelance teachers, 10

General communication skills, 6, 88-89
General English learners, 15
General English methodology, 15
General English programmes, 15
General English trainers, 15
General language knowledge, 6, 88
General management, 28
General management vocabulary, 180-181
Genre analysis, 37
Giving feedback, 110
Grammar, 35-36
Group teaching, 117-120
Guidelines on giving feedback, 116

Hard ESP, 8
Holding company, 19
Honey and Mumford, 108-109
How to delegate, 78
Human relations movement, 22-23
Human resources vocabulary, 185

In-company teachers, 10
In-service learners, 12
Institute of Commercial Management Certificate, 167
Institute of Commercial Management Diploma, 167
Inter-departmental liaison committee meeting, 53
Internal audit, 30
Internationalisation of business, 80

Checklists

Interpreter training style, 126
Interview assessment, 95
Interviews with trainees, 94

Job and career information, 154

Key issues in management, 28

Language books, 157
Language competence, 13
Language in writing, 66
Language knowledge, 5, 6, 12, 35, 88
Language of meetings, 50
Language of negotiations, 60
Language of presentations, 44
Language of telephone calls, 56
Language schools, 11
Layout in writing, 65
Leadership, 69-71
Leadership and communication, 71
Leading, 28
Learners of Business English, 12
Learning styles, 108-109
Legal, 30
Legal Department, 27
Legal vocabulary, 181
Length of time per objective, 102
Licensor-licensee negotiations, 62
Listener training style, 125-126
Listening, 89, 93
Listening books, 157
Looking at the past, 133
Looking to the future, 133-134

Management accounting, 30
Management knowledge, 13
Management needs, 13-14
Management Science, 24

Management skills, 7, 13
Managing Director, 26, 27
Manner in telephoning, 56
Manual of Learning Styles, 108-109
Manufacturing sectors, 34
Marketing Department, 27
Marketing vocabulary, 181
Marketing, 9, 30
Maslowis hierarchy of needs, 23
Materials organisers, 159
Mecson, Albert and Khedouri, 20
Medium of materials, 129-130
Meetings, 43-54, 107
Meetings course programme, 51-52
Meetings evaluation, 113
Meetings language, 171-175
Meetings skills, 49
Mind Your Manners, 81
Model group course report, 148-150
Model individual course report, 146-147
Model lesson plan, 105
Model plan for communication practice, 137
Model plan for language study, 135-136
Mole, John, 81-82
Multimedia and PC, 159
Multimedia materials, 130

National culture, 82
Needs analysis, 87-97
Negotiating skills, 59
Negotiations, 57-63
Negotiations language, 176-180
Negotiations models, 58

Objectives of a meetings course, 50
Objectives of a negotiations course, 57
Objectives of a presentations course, 45

Objectives of a telephone skills course, 57
Objectives of Business English, 4
Objectives of writing courses, 64-65
Observation of trainees, 95
One-to-one teaching, 117-120
Open evaluation led by trainer, 140
Open group courses, 89
Organisations in business, 18
Organising, 28
Oxford International Business English Certificate, 163-164

Pacing, 121
Partnership, 19
People in meetings, 49
People in negotiations, 59-60
Personnel, 9, 30
Personnel Department, 27
Phrases for secretaries minuting meetings, 174
Planning a lesson, 104-108
Planning and procedures in negotiations, 60
Planning, 28
Pragmatist learning style, 108
Preparation of telephone calls, 56
Presentations, 43-47, 106
Presentation evaluation, 112
Presentations course programme, 45-46
Presentations language, 169-171
Pre-service learners, 12
Principles of effective presentation, 47
Print materials, 130
Private limited company, 19
Problem-solving meetings, 48
Procedures at meetings, 49
Procedures for chairpersons, 51

Procedures for participants in meetings, 51
Procedures for secretaries at meetings, 51
Production, 30
Production and operations vocabulary, 181
Production Department, 27
Professional associations, 154
Professional communication skills, 6, 89
Professional content, 17
Professional context books, 158
Professional development, 155
Professional press, 154
Programme outline, 102-103
Public limited company, 18
Publishers, 155-156
Purchasing Department, 27
Purchasing, 30
Purchasing vocabulary, 186-187

Qualifications, 154-155

Raw versus published materials, 127-128
Reading, 89, 93
Reading books, 159
Reflector learning style, 108
Research and development, 32, 33
Research and Development Department, 27
Research and development vocabulary, 181
Results in negotiations, 60
Results of meetings, 49-50
Reviewing the course, 139

Sales, 32
Sales Department, 27
Sales vocabulary, 181
Sample self-study programmes, 134-137
Scientific management, 20
Scope of Business English, 1, 5
Scope of materials and equipment, 127-131
Self assessment, 92
Service sectors, 34
Sharing control, 124-125
Soft ESP, 8
Sole trader, 19
Speaking, 89, 93
Specialist language knowledge, 6, 88
Spoken English for Industry and Tourism, 166-167
Staffing, 28
Stages in a lesson, 106-108
Standards in writing, 63
Steps in delegation, 78
Structure of a presentation, 44
Structure of telephone calls, 56
Style in writing, 66
Subsidiary company, 19

Taylor, Frederick W., 20
Teachers of Business English, 10
Teaching / training cline, 17
Teaching or training, 121-126
Team building and communication, 75
Team building, 71-75
Team development, 73-74
Telephone building blocks (called), 55

Telephone building blocks (caller), 55
Telephoning language, 175-176
Telephoning, 54-57
Text-based sources for materials, 160
The New State, 20
Theorist learning style, 108
Timing of feedback, 114-115
Trainee behaviour, 118
Trainee briefing, 102-103
Trainee contributions, 118-119
Trainee expectations, 118
Trainee involvement, 118
Trainee level, 119
Trainee objectives, 119
Trainee-controlled activities, 124-125
Trainer approaches, 119-120
Trainer characteristics, 120
Trainer-controlled activities, 124-125
Training approaches, 120
Training organisations, 11
Training styles, 12127
Treasury, 30
Trust and delegation, 76-77

Varieties of English, 36
Variety of features in writing, 66
Video, 130, 159
Video sources for materials, 161
Vocabulary, 37-38
Vocabulary books, 157-158

Ways of working of trainer and trainee, 102
Writing, 89, 93
Written documentation, 63-67